AMERICA'S HOPE

In Troubled Times

Kelly Wright

America's Hope
Copyright © 2010 by Kelly Wright

Unless otherwise noted, all Scripture references are from *The Holy Bible, New King James Version,* copyright © 1979, 1980, 1982, 1990 by Thomas Nelson, Inc., Nashville, Tennessee. References marked "NIV" are from *The Holy Bible, New International Version,* copyright © 1973, 1978, 1984 by International Bible Society, Colorado Springs, Colorado. References marked "MSG" are from *THE MESSAGE,* copyright © 1993, 1994, 1995, 1996, 2000, 2002 by NavPress Publishing Group, Colorado Springs, Colorado. References marked "NLT" are from *The Holy Bible, New Living Translation,* copyright © 1996, 2004, 2007 by Tyndale House Foundation. Used by permission of Tyndale House Publishers, Inc., Carol Stream, Illinois.

All rights reserved. No part of this book may be reproduced or transmitted in any form or by any means, electronic or mechanical, including photocopying and recording, or by any information storage and retrieval system, without permission in writing from the publisher.

McDougal Publishing is a ministry of The McDougal Foundation, Inc., a Maryland nonprofit corporation dedicated to spreading the Gospel of the Lord Jesus Christ to as many people as possible in the shortest time possible.

Published by:
McDougal Publishing
P.O. Box 3595
Hagerstown, MD 21742-3595
www.mcdougalpublishing.com

ISBN 978-1-58158-155-3

Printed in the United States of America
For Worldwide Distribution

Dedication

I dedicate this book:

To my lovely wife, Loretta
To my sons, Mychael and Morgan
To my daughter, Sarah
To the memory of my mother, June Lorraine Overton,
   who guided me with loving care. Her pearls of wisdom and faith in God resonate within my heart and
   soul every day that I live. Thank you, Mom.

How often we fail to fully appreciate the heroic efforts of the brave men and women who voluntarily serve in the branches of the U.S. military. For many who are serving in harm's way, political ideology stops at the end of the spear. These men and women are united in their effort to engage and overcome America's enemies on the battlefields of Iraq and Afghanistan. They are on the front lines trying to prevent another 9/11-type of terror attack on the United States. They are trying to stop the slaughter of innocent people throughout the world. They are trying to defend the ideals of democracy and freedom that we cherish here in the United States. Their task is not easy, but they realize they are a vital part of *AMERICA'S HOPE*.

From the Journal of Kelly Wright

Contents

How wonderful it is, how pleasant when brothers
   live together in harmony!
For harmony is as precious as the fragrant anoint-
   ing oil that was poured over Aaron's head, that
   ran down his beard and onto the border of his
   robe.
Harmony is as refreshing as the dew from Mount
   Hermon that falls on the mountains of Zion.
And there the LORD has pronounced his blessing,
   even life everlasting.   Psalm 133, NLT

"I'm praying not only for them
But also for those who will believe in me
Because of them and their witness about me.
The goal is for all of them to become one heart and
   mind—
Just as you, Father, are in me and I in you,
So they might be one heart and mind with us.
Then the world might believe that you, in fact, sent me.
The same glory you gave me, I gave them,
So they'll be as unified and together as we are—
I in them and you in me.
Then they'll be mature in this oneness,
And give the godless world evidence
That you've sent me and loved them
In the same way you've loved me."
                              John 17:20-23, MSG

Introduction

Here you are, going through the blues and blahs of what we sometimes call a "bummer life." Your sense of rejection continues to make you feel like your life is totally out of control. And here I am, writing about your life, with yet another self-help book, another book about hope, another look at your problems. You might be saying, "That's just what I need! Another person who thinks he knows it all, telling me how to live my life! No, thank you! I can be miserable or live poorly all by myself! I've had my fill of you Holy Rollers, you Joel Osteen, Anthony Robbins, Les Brown, and Willie Jolley wannabes!"

Well, stop right there! I'll be honest with you. I do like the positive message of such luminaries among the lot of modern motivational/inspirational speakers, but let's make one thing abundantly clear. I am not a counselor, life coach, economist, financial planner, therapist, psychologist, or guru. I am a journalist, which means I broadcast and report news—good and bad. I am also an ordained minister, which means I am called by God to deliver the good news to a world filled with bad news.

However, and more importantly, the fact of the matter is

that I'm just like you, a person living in a world that's spinning out of control. And, like you, I'm trying to hang on and overcome. I'm determined to emerge victorious over life's problems.

Do I have all the answers? Of course not. But I've learned a lot through my own struggles, through my observation of life here and abroad and through listening to and reading from great men and women who do have proven answers. One thing I know: There is hope for America and the world, and I request your indulgence as I attempt to give you some simple and proven answers for our troubled times. This, my friends, is *America's Hope*.

Kelly Wright
Hagerstown, Maryland

Chapter One

Heal the Man, Heal the Land

Explosions rip through the heart of the city, inflicting pain and casualty.

A cowardly act of despicable terror increasing fear and misery.

Your wounded heart, so bruised and battered, tearing apart at the seams.

Your shallow life, so torn and tattered, filled with regrets and broken dreams.

Lord, we need salvation. Please come and heal our nation.

Lord, we need deliverance. Please come and give us forgiveness.

What the world needs now is love, because there's just too little of.

It's so crazy the way we're living our lives.

It's so insane; this kind of living ain't right.

In times like these, do you ever wonder? Could it be we need a savior? —— SAVIOR by Kelly Wright

Isn't it a shame? For all of our great exploits, discoveries, inventions, and successes, we humans still find ourselves unable to build a lasting peace among our neighbors in the world. Why is that? What keeps us constantly embroiled in warfare, violence, and unrest, divided by race, class, and gender? Why does hope seem to be so elusive?

Take a look around, watch the news on television, listen to a news brief on the radio, read a newspaper, or go online to search the news, and the result is the same. Whatever you are reading, listening to, or watching, you are certain to be bombarded with reports that tell you that our world is crumbling beneath the weight of financial downturns, war, terrorism, bloodshed, violence, government and corporate corruption, poverty, genocide, homicide, suicide, racial and ethnic divisions, and global warming. All of these maladies can lead us to feel helpless, with a loss of trust and a feeling of insecurity. We seem to be dangling from our last thread of hope.

Think about this. If you're an adult living in virtually any part of the industrialized, computerized, and so-called civilized world, by now you know the drill. Chances are you get up in the morning with a mind filled with what you worried about all night. How far has the Dow dropped? How much money have you lost in your 401-K? How are you going to pay for your children to finish college? Can you keep your home from going into foreclosure? Help! You sigh, "Oh, what am I going to do?"

These are the same thoughts that rocked you through

another restless night of sleep. Awakened by your burdens, you now drag yourself through another day, plagued by the anxiety of uncertainty. Still, you dream about something that will somehow alter your condition and turn your drab reality into a thing of beauty.

You ask yourself the question: Did my lottery ticket win this time? Have I finally struck it rich? And you daydream about how all those millions of dollars might greatly change your world. As your false hope builds, your mind dwells on grand illusions. You see yourself as a successful person, able not only to pay all your bills, but even to lavish expensive gifts on your loved ones, pay for their college, buy an upscale house and luxury cars, and travel the world. It all seems so real you can almost taste it, but then the true reality slaps you in the face, and you awake from your daydream and are faced with the harsh truth that your circumstances haven't changed a bit. Depressed and downhearted, you sink back

> *Our world is crumbling beneath the weight of financial downturns, war, terrorism, bloodshed, violence, government and corporate corruption, poverty, genocide, homicide, suicide, racial and ethnic divisions, and global warming.*

into your miserable doldrums and silently moan that your situation is "hopeless."

You may be looking for a turnaround in your health. Cancer, AIDS, heart failure, or some other ailment or disease may be keeping you flat on your back. In your heart, you're praying for someone to offer you encouragement, but the grim faces of your doctors, nurses, and loved ones paint a picture of hopelessness. Your life is drifting away from you, and there's nothing you can do to hold on to it. Instead, you helplessly watch it drift, like a puff of wind or the steam from a tea kettle disappearing into the air. So there you are, feeling like it's just a matter of time before you check out of this big experiment called life.

You think to yourself, "Was it worth it? Am I better off having lived and loved? Did I help anybody along this journey? Will my loved ones, friends, or anybody at all miss me when I'm gone? Does anybody really care? What awaits me beyond death? Will I wake up in heaven or in hell?" In fact, you wonder aloud, "Why don't I know the answers to these questions? Have I lived my life totally ignorant of God? And will He even hear me now?"

Maybe you are feeling like you've wasted far too many years of your life in a marriage that you now consider to be wrecked. You're tired of her yelling at you about how stupid you are, and you're wondering why in the world you married her in the first place. You say to yourself, "I thought this was the girl of my dreams, but, boy, was I wrong. Besides," you reason, "it seems pretty clear that she doesn't love me or know how good a man I am. Otherwise, she wouldn't be starting all of these silly arguments."

You think to yourself that your marriage is "hopeless." The relationship has fallen, and there seems to be no way for it to get back up. So you're determined to look elsewhere, to seek a more meaningful and fulfilling relationship with a woman who really appreciates you, a woman who will make you feel good about yourself. You're tired of all the marital warfare.

If you're a woman, look at yourself. You're beautiful, but you feel like an ugly duckling because you can't find a good man who will treat you like a lady. You're in and out of relationships with men who offer you very little respect. Chivalry is dead, the men you date treat commitment as if it were a dirty word, and communication is a one-way conversation that always seems to center on them. You mull over the choices you've made in life in regard to relationships, and you begin to experience those sinking, sagging, and nagging thoughts that you're a woman who has failed in life simply because you're alone. It seems that all of your girlfriends are involved in relationships, while you're all by yourself. You have no one to date and no prospects of ever getting married. You can't find a good man or keep a good man, and you just feel so lost and alone. Come to think of it, there are times when you look at yourself in the mirror and sigh, "What's wrong with me?"

These are but a few of the internal struggles that people contend with on a daily basis in our modern world. Far too many are walking through life with a façade that says that everything is great, but, at the same time, they're living their lives in constant fear of impending doom. You know the feeling all too well. Your daily living is filled with turmoil, pain, and misery. You have tried talking to friends about your situation, only to discover that your friends can't console you because they have problems of their own, and sometimes they're even worse off than you. Furthermore, some of those so-called friends are telling other friends about your situation, and now all of your business is out on the street through gossip, rumor and innuendo. What a mess!

Some of us have even opened up to pastors, counselors, loved ones, or therapists and been disappointed. In the case of opening up to pastors, the next time we went to church on a Sunday morning, we received funny looks from certain church members. When the pastor began to preach his sermon, we began to recognize certain code words in what he was saying, and suddenly it dawned on us that he was talking about us, broadcasting

> *You have tried talking to friends about your situation, only to discover that your friends can't console you because they have problems of their own, and sometimes they're even worse off than you.*

our circumstances to the entire congregation. As we sank deeper into the pew, we rationalized that at least he wasn't identifying us by name, but that didn't stop us from feeling mortified and betrayed by someone we trusted to keep our problems concealed and private. We feel angry and hurt that our life's story is now being used as a Sunday-morning sermonic lesson on just how messed up our lives can become in these days.

As for the therapist and counselor, you put their plan to work and, like a good soldier, you march on, implementing their philosophy or strategy into your battle plan for winning the war against your dilemma. Every day you try harder and harder to engage the enemies and demons of your life, only to find yourself falling into an ever-deepening abyss.

Think about it. People are living wild and crazy these days, and that can drive anyone insane. I'm striving, just like you, not to go mad and lose my mind in this world gone mad. And, I'm sure, you, too, are living your life in the maddening melody of being on the edge, as the old-school hip-hop rap song goes: "Don't push me, 'cause I'm close to the edge. I'm trying not to lose my head. It's like a jungle sometimes. It makes me wonder how I keep from going under" (Grandmaster Flash).

Our life today in the twenty-first century is indeed a life on the edge, a life in the jungle. There seem to be no more rules of civility. It's just a fight for survival. We often ask ourselves, "Can I make it through another day?" Can you start and end your day without getting sucked into depression over your finances, frustration with your employer (who failed to give you the raise you think you deserve), the anger you feel over losing your job (How do you take care of your family now or pay the bills?), or having that feeling that life just "sucks."

Former President Bill Clinton once said, "I feel your pain." Well, not only do I feel your pain; I know your pain. Just like you, I'm living through it. In my own feeble attempt to illustrate just how in tune I am with your life, allow me to be very transparent with you. I've been homeless, unemployed, broke, divorced, brokenhearted, robbed at gunpoint, fired, laughed at, talked about, ridiculed, persecuted, misunderstood, flimflammed, bamboozled, and scorned. Oh, and did I mention that there have been plenty of times when I've been downright wrong, making some pretty stupid decisions, poor choices that set me up for failure instead of success?

Now you're really saying to yourself, "I have nothing to gain by reading a book by this idiot. What can I learn from a loser like Kelly Wright?" Well, perhaps nothing, but please do read on. After all, what do you have to lose? Don't close the book just yet. I want you to know that all the book of my life has not yet been closed. There are still more chapters left for me to live.

This is not my life's story; that is a subject for a later book. Right now, I want you to understand that, just as I did, you can overcome any challenge or obstacle that confronts you. Your life is not over because of some current mistake or failure in your distant past. There are certainly more new editions to be added to your life. And when those chapters are added, I have faith that God will provide you with a victorious ending.

Let's agree to pore over these pages together and discover what keeps us smiling in the midst of setbacks, what keeps us upbeat in the face of economic downturns, what keeps us positive when so many circumstances are so negative, and what keeps us hopeful that life will always be good, when the world is staged to produce so many things that are bad.

From the start, I should warn you that this is not a book about prosperity. You will find no get-rich-quick schemes here or formulas for positive thinking. It is merely a book based on my faith that, despite failure, setbacks, and seemingly insurmountable odds, God faithfully provides a way out when there seems to be no way for me to overcome whatever obstacle I am presently facing. He provides the tools for me to find healing, reconciliation, and restoration. He enables me to develop a winning attitude that says: "I am victorious!" and *"I can do all things through Christ who strengthens me"* (Philippians 4:13).

There's no doubt about it. The people of the world are groaning beneath the weight of their circumstances—whether it's suffering from the devastating effects of a global economic meltdown, facing foreclosure, dealing with unemployment, desperately seeking a job (just to keep food on the table), or trying to stay alive in a war-torn environment like that of Iraq or Afghanistan (where terrorists and insurgents unleash furious attacks on innocent people). Consider the millions of refugees who are trying to survive in the Sudan (where many have been killed as victims of genocide) or the people in other remote regions of the globe who are struggling to overcome poverty. There is a desperate need for healing everywhere.

How, in a world gone wrong, do we find a way to get it right? Or, more importantly, how do we make ourselves right for the world in which we live? Many of you may scoff and say, "That's impossible and impractical!" In many ways, you scoffers, critics, and cynics have a valid point. Your argument is based on solid evidence which shows that some people refuse to accept help to break the bonds of enslavement to an impoverished life.

There are a number of reasons why such conditions exist; among them are poor education, lack of medical help, inadequate funding for building a community's infrastructure (such as schools, homes, and farms), and even a vicious cycle of generational failure. God Himself has something to say about all of these things:

> *My people are destroyed for lack of knowledge.*
> Hosea 4:6

> *For lack of guidance a nation falls, but many advisers make victory sure.* Proverbs 11:14, NIV

Heal the Man, Heal the Land

Let's take a look, for a moment, at the root of any person's problems. It's our thoughts. That's right, our minds can wreak havoc upon our lives. Like a whirlwind that stirs up dust and debris, our thoughts can spiral out of control with negative messages that can wreck the very image we have of God and ourselves. When this happens, we become susceptible to having our poor thoughts manifest themselves in poor decisions about every aspect of our lives. We can actually sabotage our plans, short-circuit our prayers to God, abuse our relationships with family and friends, and just make a general mess of things. And all of this stems from crazy, stupid thoughts swirling around in our minds.

How, in a world gone wrong, do we find a way to get it right? Or, more importantly, how do we make ourselves right for the world in which we live?

It's been said that thinking makes the person. It's not the clothes we wear, the car we drive, the house we own, or the money we earn. Thinking definitely makes the person. God agrees with this assessment. He said, *"For as he thinks in his heart, so is he"* (Proverbs 23:7).

Our thoughts are the beginnings of who we are. They produce the actions we take, and, for that reason, they can lead to either life or death. There are thoughts within our minds that can produce negative results, and there are thoughts that can produce positive results.

When problems come our way, we have the tendency to run and hide rather than face things head-on. The hiding places we choose, however, offer us no real way of escape. They only shroud us in a deeper darkness. Then, like a python or a boa constrictor, our problems wrap themselves around us and squeeze us tighter and tighter, until we can no longer breathe. In this way, our circumstances crush the very life out of us. Unless we can find a way to deal with our problems, they will suffocate us and cause us to die an early death. At the very least, they will cause us to let slip our desire to live life to the fullest, weathering every storm by being anchored to a foundation of indomitable faith.

I find that it's often better to confront a problem as it presents itself. Putting a problem off only allows it to fester and become a greater burden. This, in turn, causes us to become anxious and to perceive the problem as being bigger than it really is, the very biggest obstacle in our lives. How do we deal with an issue that will not change by worrying and struggling? Problems can only go away through direct response, taking wise action to combat them and overcome them before they grind us to a pulp or lead us to commit some desperate act.

Two recent incidents reflect the extreme nature of losing hope, losing faith, and losing one's mind. In my home state of Maryland, a young husband and father, facing what appeared to be insurmountable debt, took the time to write four suicide notes and then proceeded to slit the throats of his wife and three small children, before taking his own life. In another incident, things went horribly wrong for a family from Long Island, as they were visiting their daughter in college. In the hotel where they were all lodged, the father took the lives of his wife and two daughters, before killing himself. He left no note behind, but police speculated that the cause of his twisted decision to end his family's life and his own was his financial woes. He had allegedly swindled others out of millions of dollars. How tragic each of these cases is.

What's so alarming is that there are more incidents like these that sometimes go unreported. These are painful reflections of the times in which we live. They are also indicators that some people are basing all of their hopes and dreams on things that cannot produce true happiness and fulfillment. Money, gold, homes, and material wealth will fade away. They can never provide the love and caring support that sustains hope in perilous times.

Moved by these unfortunate sets of circumstances, I wrote a song hoping to encourage people to become more observant of what their neighbors or co-workers might be going through and to get help for them if they're showing symptoms that something isn't quite right. Is their outward show of anxiety, depressions, or unhappiness (or even over-happiness) only masking some inner pain?

America's Hope

Man shoots his wife, his daughter, and then his son,
Then takes his own life with the very same gun.
He lost his job, life was too hard ... or so he believed.
Too bad he didn't stop for a moment to pray.
He would have found a better answer that day.
He'd have found release and gained some peace.
Instead, he was deceived.

> Everyone is in need of help, for no man is an island; therefore, we should all become our brother's keeper.

Please, can we help them when they're crying through the night?
We've got to help them when there's no help in sight.
Please, can you help them when their lives are filled with fright?
We've got to help them to step into the light.

All through the night she walks the streets alone.
She's got three kids to feed, living at home.
She sells her body to get some money, to keep them off welfare.
A homeless man, he begs for some food to eat.
Nobody sees him, as they pass by the street
Where he lies dying. A preacher's crying,
"Can you help, somebody, please?"

Heal the Man, Heal the Land

Please, can we help them when they're crying
through the night?
We've got to help them when there's no help in sight.
Please, can you help them when their lives are filled
with fright?
We've got to help them to step into the light.
— HELP by Kelly Wright

Everyone is in need of help, for no man is an island;
therefore, we should all become our brother's keeper. I find
help in dealing with my problems by searching the truths
and wisdom of the Bible. Within its pages are examples of
how to defeat any foe and overcome any obstacle. Reading
the sacred Scriptures allows me to take on a higher level of
thinking, one that is contrary to humanity's stale and ob-
solete way of dealing with issues. I find that without God
we become mired in chaotic "stinkin' thinkin'," while God
is involved in a level of thought that sheds light on any issue, exposing it under the light of truth and providing an
eventual breakthrough:

People with their minds set on you, you keep com-
pletely whole,
Steady on their feet, because they keep at it and
don't quit.
Depend on God and keep at it because in the Lord
God you have a sure thing. Isaiah 26:3-4, MSG

God makes a direct appeal to us to turn to Him in times of trouble. He has the answers we need.

Now, I know what some of you are thinking: "Oh, great! Here's another Christian who believes he has all the answers to life's questions! Here, again, is one of those Holy Rollers from the religious Right who's trying to impose his beliefs on me!" Don't give up on me just yet. I'm not a Right-winger, and neither am I on the Left. I don't believe God is either a Republican or a Democrat. Tony Evans, a well-known minister who pastors a church in Dallas, Texas, expresses my sentiments precisely: "God doesn't need an elephant [Republican] or a donkey [Democrat] to do His job. He needs ordinary people, like you and me, to do some extraordinary things that He calls us to do."

So hear me out. Our thoughts can be very toxic, if we shape them and mold them around what the world pours into our imaginations. But God, who loves us, offers a better idea. If we open our minds to understand, our ears to hear, and our eyes to read His Word and see it manifested, we can learn how to deal with any situation. For example, in Isaiah 55:6-11, He issues this challenge:

> *Seek the LORD while he may be found; call on him*
>   *while he is near.*
> *Let the wicked forsake his way and the evil man his*
>   *thoughts.*
> *Let him turn to the LORD, and he will have mercy*
>   *on him, and to our God, for he will freely pardon.*

Heal the Man, Heal the Land

*"For my thoughts are not your thoughts, neither are
your ways my ways," declares the* LORD.
*"As the heavens are higher than the earth, so are
my ways higher than your ways and my thoughts
than your thoughts.*

*As the rain and snow come down from heaven, and
do not return to it without watering the earth
and making it bud and flourish, so that it yields
seed for the sower and bread for the eater, so is my
word that goes out from my mouth: It will not
return to me empty, but will accomplish what I
desire and achieve the purpose for which I sent
it."*
                                                        NIV

In other words, God is saying that He has a better plan
for all of us. But here's the problem: We're too proud of our
puny positions on the earth, and we don't have time for
God, let alone time to listen to what He has to say about
our condition. Some people reason that God is too busy
with the universe or too detached from His creation to deal
with us anyway. Worse yet, some of us allow ourselves to
believe that there is no God, believing instead that man is
responsible for his own destiny. Here's a news alert to all of
my friends who are atheists and who defiantly proclaim, "I
don't believe in God": He doesn't believe in atheists. Hmm!
Think about *that* for a moment.

How foolish of us to go it alone through life, when God
provides us with His manifold wisdom so that we can go
through life with boldness and confidence. Consider this:

God's thoughts and ways reflect His desire to make us grow and flourish in life. He provides a full guarantee that He will make provision for us to accomplish what His Word says for us.

What I absorb from Scripture is that God is concerned about my thoughts, my cogitation or process of thinking, and He wants to redesign my form of reasoning to His ways or ideas. He wants me to forsake worldly thoughts, which result in actions that can disrupt the progress He's preparing for me. These are the thoughts that, over a lifetime, can lead me to make wrong choices, leading to actions that will produce toxic consequences of pain and trouble for me and those who rely on me—my wife and family, my friends, my co-workers, and my employer.

The inspirational author Frank Outlaw writes about the reasons that thoughts have so much meaning and value in our lives: "Watch your thoughts; they become your words. Watch your words; they become your actions. Watch your actions; they become your habits. Watch your habits; they become your character. Watch your character, for it will become your destiny."

Have you considered how your thoughts, words, and actions can help or hinder your destiny? Do you even have any idea what your true destiny is? The dictionary defines *destiny* as "the inevitable or necessary fate to which a particular person or thing is destined; one's lot." A second meaning of this word *destiny* is "a predetermined course of events considered as something beyond human power or control." *Destiny* is also defined as "the power or agency thought to predetermine events: *'Destiny brought them together.'* "

So, is it your destiny to live a life of despair, poverty, and failure? Absolutely not! Remember what God says: *"My ways* [are] *higher than your ways, and My thoughts than your thoughts"* (Isaiah 55:9). God provides us with His perfect plan to fulfill our destiny. With God, destiny is not a matter of chance, beyond our control, and neither is it unattainable. God plans for us to become rich in godly character, filled with His Holy Spirit, and filled with His grace and mercy that inspires us to tell the world about His amazing love for all mankind. In Jeremiah, God says, *"For I know the plans I have for you,"* says the LORD. *"They are plans for good and not for disaster, to give you a future and a hope"* (Jeremiah 29:11, NLT). Jesus tells us, *"I have come that they may have life, and that they may have it more abundantly"* (John 10:10).

> *God provides us with His perfect plan to fulfill our destiny. With God, destiny is not a matter of chance, beyond our control, and neither is it unattainable.*

Because of the hope God offers, we must dare to dream, dare to have visions, and dare to declare that, with God on our side, we cannot fail. Through Him, we can make our dreams a reality.

Having this hope and inspiration does not make us immune to adversity or obstacles. We *will* go through trials, tribulations, and sad times in the pursuit of holiness and happiness. But if we are wise and hold on, persevere, and endure with love, we will experience triumph. We will be able to joyfully sing the praise song: "I'm So Glad That Trouble Don't Last Always."

I am strengthened and heartened by the joy God gives me each time I rise from my slumber to face another day. Because of that, I make an effort to ensure that my first thought of the day is about Him. I begin each day thanking Him for creating me and giving me the ability to enjoy my life. I pray, "Good morning, Lord. Thank You for waking me up this morning."

Lately, I've been saying a prayer that Jabez made to God centuries ago. He prayed, *"Oh, that You would bless me indeed, and enlarge my territory, that Your hand would be with me, and that You would keep me from evil"* (1 Chronicles 4:10). I add to this, "Lord, I ask that You help me bring You glory today in the things that I do. I pray that You bless my family, friends, co-workers and bosses, world leaders, and people throughout the world."

It's important to realize that the prayer of Jabez came forth from a man whose name literally meant "pain." The Scriptures explain that when Jabez was born, his mother was in great pain throughout the delivery, and so she named him Jabez. Can you imagine growing up having a name that means "pain"? The children and adults around you would probably say all kinds of cruel things about you. Judging by the prayer that Jabez offered to God, he must have been determined not to let his life be a reflection of his name. The beauty of his relationship with God is evident in that God heard his prayer, kept him from causing any pain to others, and enabled him to live a life that would glorify and honor Him.

So, no matter what your name is (or what other label people may have attached to you), please understand that you have been born for a purpose. God has bestowed upon you certain gifts that are uniquely yours, and they can be used to bring joy to your life, to your family and friends, and to the world around you. They can also bring glory to God.

What the story of Jabez illustrates to all of us is this: The circumstances of your birth should not matter. Before you came into this world as a baby, God had preordained that you be here for a divine purpose. Each of us has a call on our life, and God desires to see us fulfill our destiny.

I will never forget the day my mother revealed to me the circumstances under which I came into this world. I won't elaborate here on my actual birth, but I do want to share with you the shocking and troubling events that led to her becoming pregnant with me.

It was a sunny Saturday morning in the summer of 1954. The small city of Hagerstown, Maryland, nestled in the valley of the Blue Ridge Mountains, was the hub of Washington County, and on Saturdays, people would come from all corners of the area to converge on the down-town for shopping. Fortunately, this downtown shopping area was only a ten to twenty-minute walk from the main Black community of Hagerstown.

On this particular Saturday morning, my mother, who was just sixteen at the time, was excited because she was going to accompany the wife of a local pastor on a shopping trip downtown. She had been happy to befriend this woman and was hoping that their relationship would be mutually beneficial.

When she knocked on the door of the parsonage, it was the pastor who answered the door and invited her inside. At any moment, Mom expected to see the pastor's wife emerge from the living room or upstairs, so she was surprised when the pastor told her that his wife had already left for downtown. What happened next caught her totally off guard and changed her life forever. The pastor proceeded to sexually assault her. Paralyzed with fear, Mom tried to fight him off;

> *No matter what the conditions were when you were born, just like Jabez (and like me or my sister), there is a divine plan for your life. Therefore, don't dwell on the past. Instead, thrive on it, living joyfully in the present, knowing that your future is filled with promise and hope.*

when that failed, all that she could do was be still, let it happen, and then get out of there as fast as she could.

Eventually, the rape ended, and she was able to leave that parsonage and never return, but, in time, she learned that she was pregnant. Who could she confide in? Who could she tell what had happened? She reasoned that if she told the authorities or anyone else, for that matter, it would be her word against the word of a respected leader of the community, the pastor of a popular church. She chose to keep the identity of her baby's father to herself.

When my grandmother found out that Mom was pregnant, her first impulse was to send her to Nebraska to get an abortion. It was still illegal at the time, which meant that my mother would have been exposed to a potentially lethal procedure. She told me that she adamantly said to her mother, "I am keeping this baby. God is telling me this will be the only child that I will have biologically."

On March 24, 1955, just five days after her seventeenth birthday, my mother delivered me into this world at Washington County Hospital, and she was right about hearing from God. I was her only biological child. My lovely sister, who, as a baby, was abused by *her* mother, was adopted. My sister and I are thirteen years apart in age, but we are extremely close and hold our mother's memory close to our hearts. Because of Mom's faith in God, we understand our purpose in life. We know that despite the circumstances surrounding our births, we are on a God-ordained course to succeed in life, help people while we are here, and bring glory to God. So the point of this revelation is to illustrate to you that no matter what the conditions were when you were born, just like Jabez (and like me or my sister), there is a divine plan for your life. Therefore, don't dwell on the past. Instead, thrive on it, living joyfully in the present, knowing that your future is filled with promise and hope.

Oh, and by the way, let me just briefly deal with those of you who adhere to the twisted belief that single mothers are the root cause of all the trouble in the world today. I am among millions of children reared by single mothers who turned out to be very productive citizens. This was not *in spite of* our single mothers, but *because of* them. They worked tirelessly to be our source of inspiration. My mother's leadership and guidance made me the man I am today, a man of devout faith in God, a loving husband, father, and grandfather (I still find it hard to believe that I'm so fortunate to still be so young and yet have grandchildren), a television news anchor and reporter, a gospel recording artist, and someone who believes that there is something divine about helping your community, your city, your nation, and your world.

Consider Dr. Ben Carson, the world's leading neurosurgeon, who performed the first successful operation to separate vertical Siamese twins. I had the privilege of interviewing him on Fox News. Carson and his brother grew up in Detroit, Michigan. Their father and mother divorced when they were young, and they were left with their single mother, who then took on the responsibility of being the sole source of parenting that he and his brother would ever know. He recalls how he was, at one point, going down the wrong path in life, gravitating toward violence, achieving poor grades in school, and becoming a difficult child, but his mother demanded something better from both him and his brother. She worked two jobs, but still made time to check their homework.

She made it a standing order that they would have to turn the television off and read two books a week. She would check their progress with this assignment regularly. What she never revealed to those boys was the fact that she herself couldn't read. Despite that fact, for the love of her children, she kept them on the road to a better life, and she molded them into men who understood that without faith in God and in the power of prayer, they could not overcome the tough challenges that lay before them.

Ben and his brother listened to their mother and learned how to become the best that they could be. The brother is a successful engineer, and Ben is now the chair of pediatrics at Johns Hopkins Hospital in Baltimore. His incredible life was captured in a movie called *Gifted Hands*, starring Oscar-winning actor Cuba Gooding, Jr.

So, for all of you who make the claim that single mothers are the source of America's problems, I urge you to do your homework. Read about the lives of some of America's great men and women, and you'll be surprised to learn how many of them were the product of a single-parent upbringing. You can even go a step further, by visiting the homes of single mothers or spending some time with the children of single parents. You might even want to become a mentor in an organization like Big Brothers and Big Sisters of America. In this way, you can become part of the army of volunteers who are making a difference. (We will learn more about such volunteers later in the book.)

I am grateful for every day that I experience this precious gift of life, and, as I said, I begin each new day with prayer. My thoughts are then constantly focused on God as I prepare for the day with some stretching and cardio exercises (to get my heart pumping and blood flowing through my body), followed by a shower, shave, dressing, and breakfast. Before I leave the house each morning, I check on my wife and sons, saying a prayer over them: "The blood of Jesus cover you, and the grace of God protect you." Only then am I out the door.

> *Before I leave the house each morning, I check on my wife and sons, saying a prayer over them: "The blood of Jesus cover you, and the grace of God protect you." Only then am I out the door.*

It is still early dawn, and all is very quiet. Daylight has not yet pierced the sky. I can hear a bird chirping, singing a song of cheer, as if to say, "Thank You, Lord." On my drive to work, I add to my thoughts of God by listening to praise music in my car, and I do all of this before hearing the news of the day. I want the first moments of my brand-new day to be focused on God, the Giver of life, Jesus, the Lover of my soul, and the Holy Spirit, who abides within me. I say to myself, in the words of popular songs, "This is the day that the Lord has made. Therefore, this little light of mine, I'm gonna let it shine. I've got a feelin' everything's gonna be all right."

Are you free like me? *"Therefore if the Son makes you free, you shall be free indeed"* (John 8:36).

> *No captivity; I've got liberty.*
> *No defeating me; I've got victory,*
> *'Cause Christ delivered me.*
> *And I'm free indeed.*
>
> — From FREE by Kelly Wright

I'm free to love God with all my heart, mind, and body, free to love my wife and children with abundance of joy, free to live my life to the fullest, free to pursue my dream against all odds, and free to offer an encouraging word, motivation, or inspiration to all I come into contact with—because I'm free from negative and toxic thoughts.

Each of us must reach a point in our lives at which we

make every effort to help lead others by serving, helping to lift them up. The only time we should be looking down on someone is when we're helping them to get up.

This, my friends, is *America's Hope*.

Chapter Two

Each One Reach One, Teach One

It was New Year's Eve 2008, and A.J. stood there, at the rear of the church, in the last pew, spilling his life's story before total strangers. He confessed to the other congregants that his only recollection of past New Year's Eves was sleeping off his drunken stupor in some jail cell. On every New Year's Eve in memory, he had managed to get into trouble and get himself arrested.

A hulking Black man, who looked like he could have been a great linebacker in the NFL, A.J. had lived what I call a "thug life." But, while he appeared strong physically, he openly confessed that he lived in fear, always looking over his shoulder to see if anyone was approaching him from behind to do him harm.

The "thug life" is a rough life, and it can end in pain, prison, or even death. But this New Year's Eve, as he waited to celebrate the coming of the year 2009, a wonderful change was in the atmosphere.

The only person in the small sanctuary who knew A.J.'s

story was his mother, and she could not hold back the tears as her son began to speak. She could sense that something unusual was taking place in his life. She listened intently, as he continued to pour out his story.

A.J. could not understand why he was sharing with them these stories of his sordid failures, and he was struggling within himself as he delivered revelation upon revelation from his past.

He told the small group of parishioners present that night that he did not understand what was happening to him. He could not understand why he was sharing with them these stories of his sordid failures, and he was struggling within himself as he delivered revelation upon revelation from his past.

A.J. acknowledged that he had planned to be anywhere but in a church on New Year's Eve. His intent had been to go to a bar and "get a drunk on." He had gone, but it didn't work out as he had hoped.

The small hole-in-the-wall bar was dimly lit, and the smoke from cigarettes mixed with the smell of beer filled the room. It was the kind of place where he had often felt most comfortable. The thumping bass sound from the music playing pulsated through the room, and people bobbed their heads up and down, snapped their fingers, tapped their feet, and swayed their bodies from side to side to its rhythm.

A.J. was feeling good. He could see some familiar faces. As usual, the people were talking loudly but really saying nothing profound, as they enjoyed drink after drink, dance after dance. Still, as he tried to get into the party atmosphere at the bar, he sensed that something was wrong. On the outside, he was smiling and talking to the familiar faces, but on the inside he wasn't feeling the groove of the music, the smooth taste of the drinks, or the life of the party. He looked around, breathed in the smoke, and smelled the different fragrances—cologne and perfume that had become stale from sweat, smoke and liquor. On any other night, he would be enjoying every moment of this typical night in a small, dark bar, but this night he was seeing through it all and noticing that, even in a room full of people, he was feeling lonely, unfulfilled, and frustrated. The smooth taste of the liquor was failing to do its job, numb his sense of reality, and replace it with the spirit to "party hearty" all night long.

As he looked around the room, he began questioning himself: "What am I doing here? What's in this for me? Where should I be right now?" Somehow feeling like he was out of place, he left the bar and went home. But as he sat there alone in his home, the questions kept coming: "What's in this for me? Where should I be right now?"

It was New Year's Eve, and he was all alone, not what he had planned. He couldn't understand why he hadn't heard from his friends. Any other time, they would all be calling him to make plans for a party, but no one had called. He decided that he would reach out to them, only to discover that he had used up all the minutes on his cell phone. So that's why he hadn't received their calls!

But not long after he had made the discovery that he could not receive or send calls on New Year's Eve, the phone mysteriously rang. Eagerly, he picked it up and answered, only to hear the voice of his mother. She was inviting him to go to church with her for a New Year's Eve service at the tiny Bethel African Methodist Episcopal (AME) Church in Greencastle, Pennsylvania. What could he say? Spending New Year's Eve in church with his mother was not his idea of fun, but he certainly wasn't doing anything better at the moment. So, why not? He agreed to go.

The church looked like some relic from the past, and A.J. instinctively began making comparisons between it and the small bar he had left earlier. The church, like the bar, was rather small, but the church was different in that it was filled with light, whereas the bar had been very dark. In the church, there was a fragrance of sweet perfume from the pine needles on the Christmas tree that stood adorned with lights in a front corner of the church. No cigarette smoke or stale liquor odor here.

The music was simple. A woman sat at a piano playing Christmas carols, while the small group of no more than thirty men, women, and children sang along.

As the service progressed, the pastor gave people the opportunity to stand and say something. This was called the testimonial portion of the service, and A.J. was amazed by what he heard. One by one, the parishioners stood and shared their personal stories of faith, hope, and redemption, and without realizing it, A.J. gradually felt the weight of his self-doubt and frustration beginning to lighten. He found himself intently listening to each person who spoke. It was as if he was hungry for any morsel of good old down-home spiritual food to nourish his troubled and weary soul.

He heard people saying how good God had been to them. They had been subjected to every imaginable test and trial, and yet they were saying that God had delivered them from it all. They had dealt with economic downturns, unemployment, cancer, and other serious illnesses, fear of failure and of people, setbacks, hang-ups, war, politics, and just plain bad breaks. And yet, in spite of all these calamities, they testified not only to finding victory but also to experiencing joy in every circumstance. They went even further, predicting that, against all odds, they would remain overcomers in the year ahead through their abiding faith in God.

Wow! That was just too much for A.J. to take in. Suddenly he was bursting with a desire to confess to these people that each of their stories had touched his broken heart and soothed his troubled soul. Their words had been, to him, like a healing balm. Emotionally moved by each new story of triumph, he had begun to feel a stirring in his heart, and it compelled his weary mind to seize the moment and commit to a new way of thinking and a new way of living. From now on, instead of seeking happiness in his "thug life," he would seek it in God.

No one felt the earth shake that night, but somehow a mountain was moved in that tiny church. A.J. had climbed out of the depths of his despair, guided by a light called hope, delivered by the saving grace of Jesus Christ, and offered a promise of a more abundant life to come. Now he would live with joy and peace, and no longer with fear and doubt.

In this way, a small group of people expressing their faith in God helped lead a man living on the edge of life to a better way of living. They did not ask him what religion he belonged to, what his political party affiliation was, what type of job he held, or how much education he had. All they did was share their accounts of how God always provided for them, and that moved him.

Such celebrations are commonly known as watch night services. Instead of ringing in the New Year by watching the ball drop in New York's Times Square, going to parties to enjoy the merriment of a toast of bubbly and singing "auld lang syne," or launching fireworks, many of the faithful gather at churches across the world to celebrate the New Year. They do it by singing hymns of praise to God and bowing their knees to Him in prayer.

How do I know about A.J.? I was there that night, sitting in that small sanctuary known as Bethel AME Church in Greencastle, Pennsylvania, that rural hamlet just across the

Mason-Dixon, line that separates the Keystone State from Maryland. During the Civil War, the first Union soldier to be killed north of the Mason-Dixon line fell in Greencastle. Confederate forces marched through that town on their way to the Battle of Gettysburg.

The town of Greencastle was established in the 1730's, and George Washington visited there while en route to western Pennsylvania in October of 1794 to quell the Whiskey Rebellion. According to the Greencastle Chamber of Commerce, many people settled there in pursuit of religious freedom.

On this particular watch night, the freedom of faith still flourished, as a tiny band of believers gathered at Bethel Church to pray for the coming New Year. Just as their ancestors saw trouble and endured hardship on their journey to freedom, this group viewed the present-day troubles of a disastrous economy, unemployment, two wars and the war on terror as "nothing new under the sun." Their point of view was taken directly from Ecclesiastes 1:9: *"History merely repeats itself. It has all been done before. Nothing under the sun is truly new"* (NLT).

> *No one felt the earth shake that night, but somehow a mountain was moved in that tiny church. A.J. had climbed out of the depths of his despair, guided by a light called hope.*

As we sang songs of joy and hope, and then took part in the familiar tradition of testimony time, with people expressing their gratitude to God for being allowed to live in this present time, one gentleman expressed how the church needs to shine as a light of hope to a world filled with a lack of trust and confidence in government and financial institutions. He stressed that now was the time for people of faith to embrace each other, joining hands and praying for each other and the world.

We all acknowledged that we had endured many tests and trials. Yet, we reasoned, without a test we could have no testimony, and without trials we could not understand what it means to be an overcomer. We understood that such tests and trials revealed how faithful God had been in providing us with circumstances that developed within us the elements of faith, hope, and love.

I shared with the people gathered that night a message I had received via my BlackBerry from Pastor Allen of California, who provides a daily inspiration called "godsminute." On this New Year's Eve, the godsminute expressed the following inspiring message of hope: *"You crown the year with Your goodness, and Your paths drip with abundance. They drop on the pastures of the wilderness, and the little hills rejoice on every side"* (Psalm 65:11-12). The short commentary that followed explained that we should pray that 2009 would be a year filled with love, hope, and peace. I thought to myself how very timely and meaningful that message was. After all, with all that was transpiring within our global economy, our domestic politics, and the war on terror, it would seem that many were consumed with fear and doubt. This night, there was a different atmosphere building within this tiny group of people in search of a closer walk with God for the New Year.

After the initial singing of the Christmas carols, we sat there and sang without any musical accompaniment, except our voices, hands, feet, and a couple of tambourines. The simplicity of our praise penetrated the heart of A.J., who surprised all of us with his story. The pastor prayed for him, and the guest pastor proceeded to deliver a soul-stirring message about the need for people everywhere to recognize that God is real and that He is bigger than any problem we can encounter. She explained that we should not live our lives in fear, but in faith and in hope.

As I reflect on all that we, as a nation, have endured these past few years, I am grateful that God still blesses America despite our laissez-faire attitude toward Him. While we have been rocked by economic woes, bailouts, scandals, and other societal ills, we find ourselves still standing. I believe the reason for our strength rests on the solid foundation of a faithful God. While we have not always been grateful, faithful, or obedient to the God of our fathers, He has been remarkably faithful to us.

In so many ways, we have forgotten about the A.J.s of the world, those who are hungry to hear an encouraging word about faith and to see it demonstrated in the lives of people who love and trust God. Instead of becoming a reflection of the character of Jesus Christ, we have come under the insidious influence of political correctness. Not wanting to offend anyone, we compromise our values and find ourselves going along with whatever the latest trend or fad is, even if that offends the very heart of God. In the process, we have lost our ability to stand up for righteousness. The old adage is true: "If you don't stand for something, you'll fall for anything."

People appear to be standing on shaky ground, dealing with a frightening foundation of uncertainty. In the midst of the global political circus, we find ourselves caught up in a free-for-all that divides upon ideology. Some are asking, "Where does the church stand? Is God's house divided into Right and Left?" Some are claiming the church has taken a hard fall or even abdicated its responsibility to stand up for the truth. They argue that church folk have failed to suit up for battle within the culture clash and class wars. I'm thankful that on the most important night of his life A.J. encountered a people who were equipped with *"the whole armor of God."* They were living

> *Not wanting to offend anyone, we compromise our values and find ourselves going along with whatever the latest trend or fad is, even if that offends the very heart of God.*

beyond the pettiness of politics. Instead, they were concentrating on the greatness and goodness of God.

Paul admonished the early church:

> *Finally, my brethren, be strong in the Lord and in the power of His might. Put on the whole armor of God, that you may be able to stand against the wiles of the devil. For we do not wrestle against flesh and blood, but against principalities, against powers, against the rulers of the darkness of this age, against spiritual hosts of wickedness in the heavenly places. Therefore take up the whole armor of God, that you may be able to withstand in the evil day, and having done all, to stand.*
>
> *Stand therefore, having girded your waist with truth, having put on the breastplate of righteousness, and having shod your feet with the preparation of the gospel of peace; above all, taking the shield of faith with which you will be able to quench all the fiery darts of the wicked one. And take the helmet of salvation, and the sword of the Spirit, which is the word of God; praying always with all prayer and supplication in the Spirit, being watchful to this end with all perseverance and supplication for all the saints.*   Ephesians 6:10-18

Some of us within the body of Christ today have failed to equip ourselves with the full armor of God. Instead, we have languished in a lukewarm condition, with one foot in the world and the other one in heaven, thus creating an internal conflict between good and evil.

What happened in that small church in Greencastle on New Year's Eve 2008 provides a pattern for what can and should be happening throughout the whole world. A life can be changed in a moment, in the twinkling of an eye, if people of faith are willing to share their inspiring message of hope.

Let us remember that the gospel of Jesus Christ is filled with hope. It is the kind of hope that fills your heart with joy, peace, and faith—faith that you can climb any mountain, rise above any problem, persevere through any circumstance, and overcome any challenge. It is the kind of hope that should enable you to stand head and shoulders above partisan politics, vain ideologies, envy, strife, racial pride, and prejudice. Clearly, some of the most difficult challenges that the church is confronting today involve politics and race.

I am reminded of songs that Israel Houghton and New Breed sing that speak to our current circumstances. While so many people are living in fear and doubt, Israel wisely points out that we are alive at the greatest time in history. The disciples of Jesus, he says, would love to be alive in this day and age because they could spread the gospel via the Internet, cellphones, television, and radio, and they could even fly anywhere quickly and easily to accomplish the task. How true it is when he explains that we did not sneak into the earth; we were born for a purpose. God knew us before we were knitted in our mother's womb. We are a chosen generation, and we can and will change the world.

America, God is calling you to be a part of His chosen generation. The prophet Zephaniah declared:

> *"The LORD your God is with you,*
> *he is mighty to save.*
> *He will take great delight in you,*
> *he will quiet you with his love,*
> *he will rejoice over you with singing."*
>
> Zephaniah 3:17, NIV

One of my favorite songs from Israel expresses how God is singing over us and urging us to take the limits off of Him.

America, God wants you (and all the people of the world) to be able to hope again and believe again, to take the limits and restraints off of Him, so that He can be the God of your life. His desire is that every individual (Black or White, brown or yellow, Republican or Democrat, Conservative or Liberal, Christian or Jewish, Muslim or Hindu, bum or genius, thug or redneck, cool or geek, straight or gay—whatever and wherever you are in life) come to the realization that only in Him do we have salvation. If we surrender our ways to His ways, He will transform us. Our old sinful nature will fade away, and we will become brand new, adopting the very character traits of God. We will learn to place no limits and no boundaries on Him. Instead, we will allow Him to develop and increase all around us. We must stretch forth, break forth, and enlarge our territory.

Consider the present situation that America faces. The President, his Cabinet, and Congress are trying to save a restive people from economic ruin, wage two wars, fight against global terrorism, reform or improve health care, protect the environment, and find peace in the Middle East. With all due respect to President Barack Obama, his Cabinet, and members of Congress, I want them to be successful. I want Barack Obama to become one of the most respected presidents in our country's history. After all, if he does well, the nation will do well too. If he makes poor and unwise decisions, then I fear that our land of liberty, our home of the brave, may sink into an abyss from which we will not be able to escape.

So I pray for Mr. Obama, his Cabinet, and the members of Congress, and my prayer is that their success will be steeped in the Word of God, not in the vain philosophies and feeble ideologies of man. The President has expressed that he believes in Jesus Christ. I pray that he and those serving with him in government will follow God's Word, that they will be able to govern with the wisdom of God, under the guiding hand of the Holy Spirit. I pray that Mr. Obama will consider that small church experience that changed the life of A.J., as well as the church experience that the President himself claims led him to a personal encounter with Jesus Christ. It was Jesus who expressed the significance of how God can take the small things and expand them. *"If you have faith as a mustard seed, you will say to this mountain, 'Move from here to there,' and it will move"* (Matthew 17:20).

I pray that Mr. Obama, his Cabinet, the members of Congress, and all the people throughout our land will come to the realization that we all have two natures warring within us. The one desires to do good, and the other desires to do wrong. The good nature seeks to fill a person with joy and encouragement, but the bad nature seeks to be a source of trouble, always plotting something bad out of evil motives. "Which one," you might be asking, "will succeed?" The answer is: the one you feed the most.

To our President, his Cabinet, Congress, and the American people, I say that we are facing many mountains. Our faith in our institutions is undergoing cardiac arrest. At a time when we are filled with so much doubt and confusion, may I suggest that we follow A.J.'s

> *I pray for Mr. Obama, his Cabinet, and the members of Congress, and my prayer is that their success will be steeped in the Word of God, not in the vain philosophies and feeble ideologies of man.*

example and find guidance and encouragement in God, and in Him alone.

"We are witnesses and spokesmen for the God of infinite variety, boundless creativity, indescribable majesty and beauty. We hold in our possession a white-hot message of hope, a pulsating invitation to approach a living Savior" (Chuck Swindoll in *Growing Strong in the Seasons of Life*, Grand Rapids, Michigan: Zondervan Publishing House, 1983, p. 226).

Paul wrote to the church in Corinth:

> *We are therefore Christ's ambassadors, as though God were making his appeal through us. We implore you on Christ's behalf: Be reconciled to God.*
> 2 Corinthians 5:20, NIV

This, my friends, is *America's Hope*.

Chapter Three

Listen to God's Heart;
Act on Your Faith

If you listen closely, you can hear the heartbeat of America, beating however faintly beneath the deafening din of bellicose representatives in Congress, most of whom seem to spend a great deal of their time talking against each other rather than working together to get something done for the country and the people they represent. The dialogue and debate often become little more than malicious rhetoric used in an attempt to vanquish those who disagree.

The faint heartbeat of America is sometimes hard to detect amid the clamor and confusion of loud-mouthed politicians and pundits, who wage war with their words to crush those in opposition and force them to the ground. In the chambers of Congress, Liberals are always pulling to the left; Conservatives are always pulling to the right. Stuck in the middle of this great ideological tug-of-war is the heart of the American people in urgent need of care.

In this way, both Republicans and Democrats are tearing America's heart apart at the seams. With a broken heart, because of failed leadership, the American people appear to be shouting to their leaders: "Help me! I've fallen, and I can't get up." We, the people, are in need of emergency CPR (Congress Performing Responsibly). Instead, we see our elected leaders acting more like attack dogs trained to devour each other. It is extremely frustrating for the American people when they witness those whom they have elected as their representatives engaging in partisan wrangling instead of rising above the political squabble and seeking common ground on every issue, in order to effectively serve and do the will of the people.

I have seen this matter up close and personal. As a Washington correspondent and anchor for a major television network, I have conducted numerous interviews with members of Congress and political strategists from both the Republican and Democrat ranks. Lately, the tone and tenor of life inside the Beltway has sunk into a morass of disdain and contempt. It is rare for our elected leaders to find anything much they agree on, when it comes to the serious matters of growth and development in our nation. While I certainly understand their desire to hold on to their political beliefs and principles, I find it troubling that no one wants to give up any toe hold on their turf, thereby exchanging ideas and seeking some consensus on how to resolve the issues confronting this nation.

When any man or woman is called upon to serve in government, they should recognize it as a noble calling. In that position, they can help create legislation that could bring about a better way of life for millions of individuals. Our power, we must always remember, rests within the grace of God. Therefore, elected leaders must exercise humility, realizing that God is the ultimate authority.

Consider this quote:

> Government, then, is established by God. That doesn't mean that He approves of everything that governments or their representatives do. But good or bad, He chooses to allow them to exist and have authority. He actually works through them to accomplish His purposes.
>
> – From an article entitled "The High Calling of Government Service" from *The Word in Life Study Bible,* Thomas Nelson Publishers, Nashville, Tennessee: 1996, p. 566

It is rare for our elected leaders to find anything much they agree on, when it comes to the serious matters of growth and development in our nation.

How great it would be to see our government leaders come to an understanding of the noble profession of service they have chosen. Instead, I often find myself wanting to shout at them, "Please stop this madness! Can't we all just learn to get along? Can't we learn to listen to each other? Think about what you're saying to each other. Think about the hostility that you're generating. Have you forgotten that this land is your land, this land is my land, this land is *our* land?"

All of us are stakeholders in the past, present, and future greatness of this nation. Men and women serving in our military are even now dying on the battlefields of Iraq and Afghanistan. They are willing to make the ultimate sacrifice for the sake of protecting the ideals of freedom that we treasure. An excerpt from an entry in my journal, written during my visit with the troops in Iraq, reads:

> *How often we fail to fully appreciate the heroic efforts of the brave men and women who voluntarily serve in the branches of the U.S. military. For many who are serving in harm's way, political ideology stops at the end of the spear. These men and women are united in their effort to engage and overcome America's enemies on the battlefields of Iraq and Afghanistan. They are on the frontlines trying to prevent another 9/11-type of terror attack on the United States. They are trying to stop the slaughter of innocent people throughout the world. They are trying to defend the ideals of democracy and freedom that we cherish here in the United States.*

Their task is not easy, but they realize they are a vital part of America's Hope.

While working on assignment there in Iraq, I had the honor of seeing firsthand what these brave troops were doing to protect our freedoms and spread the concept of hope throughout the world. On May 15, 2004, Camp Cuervo was abuzz with activity. This Army base was located near the notorious section of Baghdad called Sadr City, a stronghold for the fiery and defiant cleric Moqtada Al Sadr. The radical cleric controlled a militia force that had been responsible for launching attacks on U.S. troops and other members of the Coalition forces.

The American men and women stationed at Camp Cuervo were members of the 2-8 Cavalry Division from their home base at Fort Hood in Texas. Their mission in Baghdad was to conduct civil affairs and humanitarian missions, but doing this task in the middle of a region of hostile forces placed them in a very precarious position. Still, each of the leaders displayed confidence that they could complete their mission. Here's an account of the group's action taken from my journal:

> *Captain Steve Gventer, a native Texan, is the kind of leader you would want on your side—athletic, good-natured, and fearless. He has a heart for people and loves accepting challenges. He's been working very hard with sheiks, clerics, and some of*

Saddam Hussein's former military generals. He's out winning hearts and minds. Critics and cynics say we are winning the battles but losing the war because the Iraqis don't like us. Tell that to the Iraqi children who run up to Captain Gventer's men to hug them when they roll through the neighborhood in their tanks and Humvees. I saw kids eagerly run to the soldiers, waving and smiling, to get candy and hugs from the troops.

Beyond this sign of hope, I walked and talked with Captain John Morning, as we literally walked among Iraqis in the popular Al-Muthana business district. I call it "marketplace diplomacy." Like a town mayor, Captain Morning tries to bring all people here together—rich, poor, Shia, Sunni, Kurdish, Muslim, Christian, Iraqi, and American. He talks with them one-on-one, in a crowd or whatever it takes, to show that America cares about the people of Iraq.

> **The Iraqi children ... run up to Captain Gventer's men to hug them when they roll through the neighborhood in their tanks and Humvees. I saw kids eagerly run to the soldiers, waving and smiling, to get candy and hugs from the troops.**

At another location, I watched Captain Morning and his troops reach out to some of Baghdad's poorest, distributing food and clothing to the families in need.

While they shared these tender moments of being charitable and hospitable to each other, across town, tragedy struck. Five Iraqis—four women and a man—who worked at Camp Cuervo had left the base in their car, not knowing they were followed by a group of militants. When they left the vicinity of Camp Cuervo, crossing the Tigris River into another section of Baghdad, the militants, who were armed with AK-47s, opened fire in broad daylight on the innocent workers, riddling their car in a hail of gunfire. The bullets hit their mark multiple times, killing one man and three women. The gunmen drove off to avoid any retaliation from police or U.S. forces. A fourth woman sustained gunshot wounds, but in a desperate act of survival managed to crawl out of the car window. People who witnessed the brazen attack cautiously rushed to her side and called for help. She was rushed back to Camp Cuervo's hospital, where doctors treated her. The U.S. military provided sanctuary for her.

Captain Morning and Captain Gventer explained to me that these kinds of attacks had unfortunately become a problem for Iraqis who worked with American or British forces. In fact, we had been

*reporting that Moqtada Al Sadr had issued an offer
of a cash reward to anyone who captured or killed
a foreigner or an Iraqi who works with them. They
were using brutal and sadistic methods to keep their
own people pinned down in fear and oppressed by
the threat of death. These Islamic militants, insurgents, and terrorists would use the barrel of a gun
rather than a ballot box, not allowing democracy to
work or letting there be a government by the people
and for the people.*

This was a day in the life of the soldiers of the 2-8 Cav
of Fort Hood, Texas, men and women humbly, yet courageously, serving their country, by helping people in a
foreign land break through the treachery of terrorism, the
roguish nature of an Islamic terror network that was trying
to divide the Iraqi people and keep them from achieving
sovereignty, democracy, and freedom. Days after that incident, I recall entering into my journal my reflections on
the violence of the militants and the resiliency and faith of
the American troops and the Iraqi citizens, who wanted a
better life than brutality and bloodshed:

May 20, 2003:
*It's a beautiful morning in Baghdad. Today, Grand
Ayatollah Ali Al-Sistani is calling on all Shiites in
the holy cities of Karbala, Kufa, and Najaf to stage
sit-ins at holy sites and shrines to protest against*

violent clashes by Moqtada Al Sadr's Mehdi Army. What a small but hopeful stroke of democracy! Yet, all that I have observed in this war is mankind's ignorance. In fact, man's ignorance is universal, prevailing all over the world. Here is a country that is trying to overcome violence and secure freedom, yet there are calloused and cold-hearted men and women who would destroy any chance of that happening by urging war instead of peace. I'm reminded of Job and his travails. Job, a faithful servant of God who had lost everything precious to him, including his family, reminds us: "For we were born yesterday, and know nothing, because our days on earth are a shadow" *(Job 8:9).*
King Solomon declared: "Since no man knows the future, who can tell him what is to come?" *(Ecclesiastes 8:7, NIV).*

Living here in Baghdad for more than a month now has opened my eyes to my own spiritual ignorance. We are all guilty of not getting to know God, Jesus, and Holy Spirit on a deeper level. Spiritual ignorance is literally causing the very same problems in our peace plans for Iraq, the Middle East, and the entire planet. "The way of peace they do not know; there is no justice in their paths. They have turned them into crooked roads; no one who walks along them will know peace" *(Isaiah 59:8, NIV).*

How sad that all governments, because they are led by humankind, have a penchant for walking blind to the truth. The same can be said of my own profession, the news media. Contrary to our own proud assumptions, we do not always get it right. We often miss the heart of the story, especially when it comes to subjects like God and faith and any mention of the name Jesus Christ.

A colleague of mine from another network saw my copy of Rick Warren's book *The Purpose-Driven Life* (Grand Rapids, Michigan: Zondervan: 2002) on my desk in our Iraq bureau. A startled look moved quickly across her face, followed by a desperate but simple question, "Who would have this kind of book here in Baghdad?"

I answered with mild amusement: "Me! The book is mine!"

Before I could say anything else, she quickly followed up on her previous question by looking at me as if scoffing, and asking almost sarcastically, "So, what's *your* purpose?"

I replied, "To live to please God and fulfill His purpose for my life, to follow Jesus Christ in every way imaginable and not be left to my own devices because mankind does a poor job in developing his own plan. Just look at where we are today." She was moved by my statement, not that I said anything profound or earth-shattering, but we both could look right outside the window and see the chaos of war. And when the battle is raging right in front of your face, at that moment there is no time for a Republican thing or a Democrat thing. There is only time for a God thing. In God alone, hope prevails. There are no atheists in foxholes!

This, my friends, is *America's Hope*.

Chapter Four

Reaching Our Youth

I have also learned that there is no room for partisanship when dealing with children standing in the need of deliverance from a painful upbringing. Thankfully, America has courageous and caring men, women, and children who are on the front lines in the war against gangs, drugs, street violence, crime, premarital sex, low-living, poor education, and a lack of hope. I have met many valiant volunteers who constantly seek to develop new and better ideas to improve our nation by serving as role models to our nation's troubled youth.

One such example of America's viable spirit of volunteerism is taking place in the heart of Statesboro, Georgia. There, people from every walk of life and ethnicity have come together to serve the children who attend the Boys & Girls Club of Bulloch County. Statesboro is the home of Georgia Southern University, which provides a great talent pool of volunteers to help children ages 6 to 18 acquire the fundamental skills that will help them pursue productive goals instead of becoming lost in the mire of crime, violence, and other social ills.

The club is considered one of the top Boys & Girls Clubs in the country, winning praise for the positive results the staff, the volunteers, and the children produce. Working under the motto "It just takes one," these clubs reach out to members of the community to invest a bit of their time to help children in need. They provide numerous opportunities for volunteers to use their skills and talents to get involved with a child and make a difference in his or her life. The volunteers provide help in mentoring, tutoring, teaching, crafts, technology, or music. Because of their efforts, the clubs have become positive places for kids and assets to the community.

Nearly two thousand children are enrolled as members of the club in Statesboro, and out of that number:

> *Teen pregnancies reduced by 50%*
>
> *Drug activity reduced by 22%*
>
> *Juvenile delinquency reduced by 13%*
>
> *School absences decreased by 87%*
>
> *GPA increased by 15%*

- 95% said the club was the best thing available in the community.
- 80% said the club staff helped them learn right from wrong.
- 52% said being involved in the club saved their lives.

Other statistical findings from the club reveals:

- Teen pregnancies reduced by 50%
- Drug activity reduced by 22%
- Juvenile delinquency reduced by 13%
- School absences decreased by 87%
- GPA increased by 15%

The club also provides training for job readiness. All of this progress is made possible by people who looked beyond race, gender, politics, and other issues in order to find common ground in meeting the needs of children, many of whom are from single-parent households. Several volunteers from Georgia Southern express the hope and optimism they gain by getting involved in the lives of the kids:

> You're doing things for the kids and, at the same time, it makes you feel good, knowing that you're doing something good.
>
> – *Kartik Reddy*

At times, I'll be down and out, just kind of drag-
ging a little bit, but when I see the kids, it gives
me a boost! It picks me up! That's why I love
coming here, just dealing with the kids.

– Grady Cone

Remember your childhood. Remember somebody had to give you an extra push. Somebody
had to let you know that you are somebody. I
watched my kids become leaders, and I know
they're going to be great products in society.

– Larmarcus Hall

These volunteers are not concerned about what brand
or stripe of politics they're wearing. Very simply, they see a
need in their community, and they're getting off the fence
or the bench to lend a helping hand. They're pumping
their lifeblood and talent into making their community
a better place by motivating and inspiring children to become the best they can be.

I will always remember and treasure the evening I visited
the Boys & Girls Club of Statesboro. Executive Director
Mike Backus invited me to deliver a keynote address for
their annual Steak & Burger Night. I was amazed to see
the level of support and attention given to the club. The
mayor, city council members, attorneys, pastors, athletic
coaches, bankers, teachers, and parents participated as volunteers, providing incredible help to the children. Each

one had a story to tell about why they saw fit to invest a few hours of their valuable time into the lives of children. The main reason they were there was because they cared. I was reminded of the old adage "Children don't care how much you know until they know how much you care."

Mike Backus approaches his mission of helping every child with the thought that each child is precious and deserves a chance to pursue their dreams. Mike shared with me several thoughts on how and why the entire community of Statesboro joins him in his efforts to help the children:

> I guess it starts with the kind of cohesiveness the community has in reaching out in anything to help the children. We did a feasibility study and learned that kids were not active outside of school. We looked at the Boys & Girls Club, which was opened in 2001, to determine what would be best to serve the children. We were involved in brainstorming meetings before we took the plunge. I remember when we first opened, people literally camped out on the lawn to sign their children up for the club. It was like a rock concert, waiting for the kids to join. It was only five dollars a year. Today it's one hundred and fifty dollars a year.
>
> The mission of the Boys & Girls Club is to enable all young people to reach their full potential as productive citizens by exposing the children

to various activities that will challenge them to grow academically and spiritually.

My philosophy is: I learn best in what I'm interested in, so we asked the kids what they were interested to learn, and then we looked at things they enjoyed doing. For instance, the kids liked fashion design, so we recruited a local seamstress to help us develop a fashion design program. Within that program, the children learn how to do math, such as multiplication, in designing their own patterns.

Musically, we discovered that most of the kids were very talented, so we helped them develop their own recording studio and taught them how to record their own projects, even write their own music and lyrics. They first had to get their project approved by staff, but then they put it all together. Also, we added a television production component that enables the children to write, develop, and produce stories about events that take place at the club. Their reports air on the local cable station.

As a result of this, the kids experience a confidence factor that is unbelievable. They feel they can do anything. We set up events for them to showcase their talents and skills. We present a teen night, and they perform; plus they participate in the community arts theatre and perform ballet. One lady designed a faith-in-motion ballet class for our children, which introduces our kids to the art of dance. They perform in public events, and the community is ecstatic about it. In all that we do, we always try to have measured outcomes.

Mike further explained that the fruit of the program is measured in the transformation of the children who enroll in the Boys & Girls Club. When Akeem first entered the club, he had some serious issues with anger and hostility. Now, after working with the staff, counselors, and clubmates, he has overcome his anger problem and is now a star honor student in high school.

For Quentin, a transformed life is a blessing. He was a young teenager who was scheduled to spend most of the rest of his teen years inside a youth detention facility. Mike appeared in court to speak on his behalf and urge the judge to give the Boys & Girls Club a chance to help him find a more productive way to live. The judge agreed, and

Musically, we discovered that most of the kids were very talented, so we helped them develop their own recording studio and taught them how to record their own projects, even write their own music and lyrics.

Quentin is now reaping the benefits of being involved in a program that cares about him and shows him a better lifestyle than gangs and drugs.

Quentin is involved in the club's Passport to Manhood program, he is president of a youth group that helps with management of the teen center, and he performs in the center's dance ensemble.

Mike Backus strongly emphasizes that America should never abandon its hope in its youth. Through his leadership at the Boys & Girls Club in the small community of Statesboro, Georgia, he and the staff are showing us all that no child should be left behind:

> What we're saying to people is this: Stop throwing lives away; we have to go the extra mile, give the extra effort, and invest in young people who are begging for opportunities. We can't afford to throw kids away. I'm not concerned about your politics; I'm concerned about the kids. I had to get beyond the stereotypes people had about the Boys & Girls Club.

Mike recalls some of the hurdles that had to be overcome before launching the club. One of the challenges involved overcoming the negative stereotypes of the children who would benefit from the program. Many people held deeply rooted perceptions that such a program could not possibly help turn around the lives of troubled youth.

Mike adds:

> We had to let them [among them, some city
> leaders] know that this was not a place for bad
> Black kids who played basketball all day and
> all night long. We had to take our show on the
> road. So we took them out to the Black commu-
> nity to meet people under the umbrella of God
> and faith. We helped them understand that they
> were not just helping us; they were helping the
> entire community.

Moved by the testimonies of the children, leaders
throughout the city have now adopted the club, volunteer-
ing their time, donating their money, and providing help
wherever they can. The fruits of their labor are noticeable
in the community spirit expressed through the children.
The Boys & Girls Club often shows its appreciation to the
city by providing help to local businesses and organizations. The teens voluntarily bus tables to help the wait staff
at area restaurants, and they serve as greeters at area stores.
It's all part of the way the children learn to give back to
the community that is helping them to grow and develop
into productive citizens. Also the children are learning how
to visualize their future by talking to the people who are
already working in the professions they want to pursue.
Working on the theme of building a stronger America
through the Boys & Girls Club, the teens have their pic-

tures taken wearing the uniform of what they would like to become—soldier, firefighter, astronaut, doctor, or nurse. This process of visualization is a unique way for the kids to see themselves as they hope to be.

Mike, hearing about his case, appeared before the judge and petitioned to take Josh into the Boys & Girls Club. The result was another teen saved from a life spent in and out of detention facilities.

After I had finished delivering my keynote address to the children, volunteers, and parents during their benefit Steak & Burger Night, a couple of the club members prepared to videotape an interview with me for their local television news report. Thirteen-year-old Josh was doing the interview and was slightly nervous as he began. I made some small talk to encourage him and make him feel comfortable. That was all he needed. From then on, he asked questions like a pro. After the interview, I thanked him and embraced him and his camera crew, telling each of them how proud I was of them and how I would keep them in prayer as they pursued their dreams. They smiled and thanked me and wished me well, as they moved on to get their story edited.

Afterward, Mike told me something astounding about

Josh. Like Quentin, Josh had also been a troubled child who was facing a lengthy stay in a juvenile detention facility. Mike, hearing about his case, appeared before the judge and petitioned to take Josh into the Boys & Girls Club. The result was another teen saved from a life spent in and out of detention facilities. Now Josh is living a life full of promise and hope.

Oh, how I wish members in the hallowed halls of Congress could remember *their* childhoods, recall how their hearts raced with glee to learn something new and exciting, how their imaginations ran wild with the unlimited possibilities and dreams that flooded their souls. Oh, how I wish our congressional leaders could come to work every day with the fresh eyes of volunteers who see problems and tackle them by rolling up their sleeves and getting involved to solve them. I wish our elected leaders could just understand the fundamental principle: "Instead of being part of the problem, be part of the solution!"

How vexing it is to see our nation's leaders acting more like roughnecks embroiled in a gang fight, stewing in rancor and discord. We are wedged into an American imbroglio, a ball of confusion from the White House to the church house, from Republican to Democrat, from Wall Street to Main Street. This malicious practice must come to an end, for a nation divided against itself cannot stand.

Let me make it very clear: I have great respect for the President and our elected members of Congress. I admire their passion for serving this country as political leaders. In fact, I make it a point to pray for them every day. The task they before them is extremely difficult. They are in desperate need of God's help and guidance. And so I ask you, Mr. President, senators and representatives:

> Can we stop dividing and conquering each other over partisan principles? Can we come to a consensus of realizing the problems we face are not Republican problems, no Democrat problems; they are American problems? Let's agree to understand that we will always have differences of opinion, but we must find common ground. That common ground should be, "Let's help America to stand united, knowing that divided we will fall."
>
> Mr. President and gentle ladies and gentlemen of the House and Senate, please be quiet and just listen for a moment. Can you hear the husband and wife expressing their fear for the future of their children? They are worried about how they're going to pay for college and keep their mortgage payment current at the same time. They realize that without a job, there is little they can do, so they're reaching out to you for help.
>
> Listen closely! Can you hear the cries of a single parent who has nowhere or no one to turn to for help, now that his or her home is in foreclo-

sure? Listen closely, and you will hear the faint heartbeat of America, pulsating with the life of this country, urging you to bring responsibility, reconciliation, transparency, accountability, and redemption to the political process. Within the soul of America there is a cry for us all to come together in one accord, as our Founding Fathers so courageously and faithfully declared:

We the people of the United States, in order to form a more perfect union, establish justice, insure domestic tranquility, provide for the common defense, promote the general welfare, and secure the blessings of liberty to ourselves and our posterity, do ordain and establish this Constitution for the United States of America.

—The Preamble to the U.S. Constitution, adopted on September 17, 1787

Every time I read this Preamble to our Constitution, I am struck by the brilliance and simplicity of the document. I am moved by the fact that men from different walks of life, from various religious denominations, and from diverse political persuasions came together at the Constitutional Convention in Philadelphia to set a proper course for America to pursue. What they accomplished was no easy task. In the process, they engaged in heated debates, collapsing into vehement arguments, but ultimately they allowed their partisan ideas to be set aside in order that the common good might prevail. In this way, the Founding Fathers placed their trust in God and formed the framework for establishing a more perfect union. It is my sincere prayer to God that our current leaders will also apply a strong sense of duty, be persevering and careful, making a steady and noble effort to preserve our domestic tranquility and provide for our common defense. We must never again retreat into the chasm of constant criticism and allow ourselves to be separated by a gulf of bitterness. We must renew our commitment to pursue with all diligence the goal of being a United States of America, not divided by our politics, race, religion, gender, or any other hindrance. It is fine to agree to disagree, but at the end of the day, let us always remember that we are America, blessed by God to be the land of the free and the home of the brave.

Now may each of us be courageous enough to stand up and be our brothers' and sisters' keepers. Wake up, America! A new day is dawning, and your best is yet to come.

This, my friends, is *America's Hope*.

Chapter Five

America the Beautiful

Completely aside from the overwhelming feeling of patriotism it evokes, "America the Beautiful" is one of my favorite songs. And, in my humble opinion, no one has sung it with more soul and passion than the late, great Ray Charles. I am still moved by this former icon, who performed the song for millions and inspired us all, at least for a moment, to forget our political persuasions and our ethnic and religious differences, to reflect on how God had shed His grace on our land. I can hear him singing it, changing the order of the lyrics to suit his interpretation of a worthy message, and then belting out the song in his gospel-tinged voice, inspiring others to join him:

O beautiful for heroes proved
In liberating strife,
Who more than self their country loved,
And mercy more than life!

America's Hope

America! America!
May God thy gold refine
Till all success be nobleness,
And ev'ry gain divine!

O beautiful for spacious skies,
For amber waves of grain,
For purple mountain majesties
Above the fruited plain!

America! America!
God shed His grace on thee,
And crown thy good with brotherhood
From sea to shining sea!

There are more lyrics to this inspiring song, but the message of these two verses should be more than enough to sharpen your focus on just how blessed America truly is, with God's grace manifested all over America, crowning it with brotherhood from sea to shining sea. Lately, however, America's good seems to have been undermined by a lack of brotherhood.

Consider some of the problems that confront us and try to rob us of the grace God has bestowed upon our nation. Instead of experiencing brotherhood, we are still sharply divided along racial, religious, and political lines. Later on, we'll take a look at some who are dealing with the issue of racism. For the moment, let's continue to discuss our divide along the lines of conservatism and liberalism.

I'm reminded of the fact that America's greatest evangelist of the twentieth century, Billy Graham, often said that any kind of *ism* was doomed to fail, and yet we have not taken his message under serious consideration. We are still divided between Republicans and Democrats, and the good we are capable of producing gets pushed aside in the partisanship of a Congress that no longer enjoys the trust of the American electorate. In fact, the approval rating for Congress has plummeted to below twenty percent.

Americans are still scratching their heads, trying to figure out why and how a do-nothing Congress, during the years of President George W. Bush's administration, managed to accept a $700 billion rescue package for Wall Street, while Main Street and the side streets of America are still reeling from a mortgage collapse. Some Americans argue that Congress bailed out the

I'm reminded of the fact that America's greatest evangelist of the twentieth century, Billy Graham, often said that any kind of ism was doomed to fail, and yet we have not taken his message seriously.

perpetrators while sacrificing the innocent, hard-working taxpayers, whose only desire is to own a piece of the American pie, to achieve and live the American dream. As I write the pages of this book, the new administration of President Barack Obama and a new Congress have approved nearly $1 trillion more to stimulate America's imperiled economy.

How did America the beautiful become so ugly, and how did the American dream turn into the American nightmare? I could go through a litany of presidential, congressional, treasury, and Wall Street gaffes that pushed our country's resources to the edge of a precarious precipice, but those reasons have been discussed by the economists, world leaders, and the media *ad infinitum*. The question now is how to move forward in the midst of turmoil, how to steel ourselves with resolve that we will persevere and endure the hardship that has befallen us all, and how to become overcomers instead of a nation that succumbs to its economic woes.

My fellow Americans, my answer, I'm afraid, may be too simplistic for many. Perhaps you might find it a bit naïve. However, even at the risk of offending you, I submit that our answer, our solution to all of these problems, rests within our power to pray, our power to believe that God can heal our land, reconcile us, restore us, and transform us into a more perfect union, into an America that is beautiful again and crowned with brotherhood. To further simplify it (even at the risk of offending some of you more), in the words of gospel music great Andraé Crouch: "Jesus is the answer for the world today. Above Him there's no other. Jesus is the way."

Consider what God said to the people of Israel in the Old Testament: *"If My people who are called by My name will humble themselves, and pray and seek My face, and turn from their wicked ways, then I will hear from heaven, and will forgive their sin and heal their land"* (2 Chronicles 7:14). Take a look around. Read your newspaper headlines. Go online and Google the news of the day. Turn on your radio and listen to the news and the talk-show hosts, and turn on your television and watch the news of the day. Everywhere you stop, look, and listen, the news is of war, violence, disease, mayhem, and murder. And don't forget the gossip of the day about the Hollywood stars. Is there any question that our world, as we know it, is in need of healing?

> *Ground zero; we've lost control.*
> *Seems all mankind is losing its mind.*
> *AIDS and plagues, road rage, air rage …*
> *We're off the page, we're off the hook.*
> *It's time to take a good look in God's Holy Book.*
> *Living in fear; so much bloodshed.*
> *There is no peace when violence won't cease.*
> *Nation against nation; and all the kingdoms too.*
> *We've got wars and rumors of wars;*
> *I tell you what God's going to do.*

America's Hope

Like a thief in the night, Christ is coming back again.
Like a thief in the night, Jesus is coming soon.
— From COMING SOON by Kelly Wright

America! America! God shed His grace on thee, and crown thy good with brotherhood from sea to shining sea!

O beautiful for patriot dream
That sees beyond the years
Thine alabaster cities gleam,
Undimmed by human tears!

America! America!
God shed His grace on thee,
And crown thy good with brotherhood
From sea to shining sea!

So let us summon a new spirit of patriotism, of service and responsibility, where each of us resolves to pitch in and work harder and look after, not only ourselves, but each other. Let us remember that if this financial crisis taught us anything, it's that we cannot have a thriving Wall Street while Main Street suffers. In this country, we rise or fall as one nation, as one people. Let us resist the temptation to fall back on the same partisanship and pettiness and immaturity that has poisoned our politics for so long.

— *An excerpt from President Barack Obama's victory speech in Chicago on November 4, 2008*

This, my friends, is *America's Hope*.

Chapter Six

Dawn of a New Era

Here lies the once great nation that huddled masses from other lands flocked to in search of something better, an opportunity to express their religious freedom. Here they sought life, liberty, and the pursuit of happiness, but now many people who call this once-great nation home are dazed and confused by the whirlwind of corruption in its financial institutions, the chaos within its government, the calamity within its anything-goes pop culture, and the loss of trust in its once-cherished and venerated core value: "In God we trust." In bewilderment, they ask, "Is the American dream dead?"

Is this what people will say in the future about our great country? Will they mock us and ridicule us, saying things like this:

- The whole concept of America was a joke. The nation was too greedy to succeed.

- Democracy was their downfall.
- The idea of one nation under God, with liberty and justice for all, failed because there was no God to protect it.

I ask you, my fellow Americans, is this to be our fate? Or are we better than this? Are we a nation of people who still believe that we are the land of the free and the home of the brave? The Scriptures tell us: *"We are hard pressed on every side, but not crushed; perplexed, but not in despair; persecuted, but not abandoned; struck down, but not destroyed"* (2 Corinthians 4:8, NIV).

As we navigate the wilderness of doubt and fear in our current economic crisis, let me remind you how, in our past, we overcame the tyranny of a hostile government through a revolution that gained our independence. We overcame the despicable practice of slavery by emancipating a people from their shackles of oppression. When we faced a great depression, we were reminded by President Franklin Roosevelt: "The only

> *I ask you, my fellow Americans, is this to be our fate? Or are we better than this? Are we a nation of people who still believe that we are the land of the free and the home of the brave?*

thing we have to fear is fear itself." When we were finding our way through the turbulent social upheaval of the 1960s (as a people who were once enslaved were now trying to gain their full citizenship through Civil Rights, to put an end to the era of segregation and attain full equality), a voice in the wilderness of that movement cried out: "I have a dream that one day this nation will rise up and live out the true meaning of its creed: 'We hold these truths to be self-evident that all men are created equal'" (Dr. Martin Luther King, Jr.).

In that movement, Dr. King led millions of people who had endured every hardship imaginable—hunger, poverty, brutality and even severe beatings that caused life-threatening injuries. These people were not gripped with fear, but remained invigorated by an all-surpassing hope that God would deliver them to a better place. Without exercising any violence, they marched for justice, following a drum major who urged the nation to understand that "One day every valley shall be exalted, every hill and mountain shall be made low, the rough places will be made plain, and the crooked places will be made straight, and the glory of the Lord shall be revealed, and all flesh shall see it together" (Dr. Martin Luther King, Jr.).

This drum major of justice was so faithful to the Lord that he was willing to die before seeing his God-given dream fulfilled. On the night before an assassin's bullet took his life, Dr. King delivered an impassioned and stirring speech in support of sanitation workers in Memphis,

Tennessee. What he told the enthusiastic crowd at the Masonic Temple would ring out louder than the shot that took his life, forever proving that our words are more powerful than bullets or bombs. Words define who we are and who we are to become. On that night, Dr. King imagined what it would be like if God allowed him to take a panoramic view of the world and all of its great civilizations. Through each journey into time, he said, "I wouldn't stop there." Instead, he asked God to give him a few years in the twentieth century in the midst of confusion, a "messed-up" world, and a sick nation.

He reminded his audience that in the dark you can see the stars shining even brighter. He urged them to develop what he called a kind of "dangerous unselfishness," explaining how Jesus used the parable of the good samaritan to show that it was a man of a different race and background who reached out to help a badly wounded stranger in need, long after two of his brethren had passed him by, not wanting to be ambushed or hurt while helping one of their own. This reveals the importance of helping those in need, regardless of their station in life.

And then, as if to provide a snapshot of his own life in the Civil Rights struggle, Dr. King began talking about the things that happened after he was stabbed in the chest in 1960. *The New York Times* reported that if he had sneezed during that first night of recovery, he would have died. Dr. King took stock of the events that had led him to this night in Memphis, and he encouraged the people to help make America a better nation and the world a better place.

In the spirit of his own "dangerous unselfishness," he stated:

> Well, I don't know what will happen now. We've got some difficult days ahead. But it doesn't matter with me now. Because I've been to the mountaintop, and I don't mind. Like anybody, I would like to live a long life. Longevity has its place. But I'm not concerned about that now. I just want to do God's will. And He's allowed me to go up to the mountain, and I've looked over, and I've seen the Promised Land. I may not get there with you, but I want you to know tonight that we, as a people, will get to the Promised Land. And I'm happy tonight. I'm not worried about anything. I'm not fearing any man. Mine eyes have seen the glory of the coming of the Lord.

The very next day, Dr. King was dead, but his dream lives on, and his vision from God about seeing the Promised Land still rings true in this twenty-first century. While America deals with new challenges, King's dream, which is deeply rooted in the American dream, can be fulfilled. But there is still much work to be done.

On January 20, 2009, nearly two million people braved

the cold temperatures to stand on the Washington Mall in the nation's capitol to see and hear the nation's first Black man to be elected to that office be sworn in as our nation's 44th President. Reflecting on the moment, Congressman John Lewis of Georgia, a close friend of Dr. King's, who marched with him and almost died after a savage beating by police during the march to Selma, Alabama (on what became known as "bloody Sunday"), explained that Barack Obama's historic rise to the presidency was a momentous event. He viewed it as a down payment on fulfilling the dream of Dr. King. But he warned that there is still much work to be done. He added that without Martin Luther King, Jr., there would be no Barack Obama. Without Martin Luther King, Jr., there would be no Black elected members of Congress.

Dr. King's eldest son, Martin Luther King III, imagined what his father would say about Barak Obama becoming President of the United States. He was sure his father would be jubilant and celebrate Obama's accomplishment, but, at the same time, he would urge all Americans to remember that there is still more work to do. He would encourage Americans to roll up their sleeves and get busy with the hard work of eradicating poverty and finding a way to diminish militarism.

Stepping into his role as President of the United States, Barack Obama told the nation, during his inaugural address:

We remain a young nation, but in the words of Scripture, *"'the time has come to set aside childish things."* The time has come to reaffirm our enduring spirit, to choose our better history, to carry forward the precious gift, that noble idea, passed on from generation to generation, the God-given promise that all are equal, all are free, and all deserve a chance to pursue their full measure of happiness.

On that day, our forty-forth president echoed the familiar theme of a "dangerous unselfishness," as he outlined the history of our ancestors who came through many toils and snares to build the foundation of this nation:

In reaffirming the greatness of our nation, we understand that greatness is never a given. It must be earned. Our journey has never been one of

> *The time has come to reaffirm our enduring spirit, to choose our better history, to carry forward the precious gift, that noble idea, passed on from generation to generation, the God-given promise that all are equal, all are free!*
> — **President Barak Obama**

shortcuts or settling for less. It has not been the path for the faint-hearted, for those who prefer leisure over work or seek only the pleasures of riches and fame. Rather, it has been the risk-takers, the doers, the makers of things—some celebrated, but more often men and women obscure in their labor—who have carried us up the long, rugged path toward prosperity and freedom. For us, they packed up their few worldly possessions and traveled across oceans in search of a new life. For us, they toiled in sweatshops and settled the West, endured the lash of the whip and plowed the hard earth. For us, they fought and died, in places like Concord and Gettysburg, Normandy and Khe Sanh. Time and again these men and women struggled and sacrificed and worked till their hands were raw, so that we might live a better life. They saw America as bigger than the sum of our individual ambitions, greater than all the differences of birth or wealth or faction. This is the journey we continue today.

And so our journey goes on into a new era, but our dream is still alive, a dream that God will deliver all of us to the Promised Land: a land flowing with love for God and love for our neighbors—even for our enemies. Perhaps such a beloved community is far beyond the comprehension and imagination of many. Nevertheless, it can be said that God is always involved in the affairs of men when He is invited to partner with them.

As Dr. King did in the past, I pray that all of us will so do now, pray that God will hear our prayer from heaven and heal our land. Where there is darkness, let His light shine bright as the evening star. Let our present nightmare give way to the beauty of the American dream. Let our current despair be replaced by hope.

This, my friends, is *America's Hope*.

Chapter Seven

Home Is Where Greatness Begins

Americans are angry, Americans are hurt, Americans are jubilant and optimistic, Americans are downcast and somber. Post-election, these are a few of the descriptions used to illustrate the conflicting mood prevailing in our nation. Are you angry? Are you sick and tired of being sick and tired? Are you fed up with Congress and the President? Are you unemployed due to the greed of Wall Street fat cats or credit-company big wigs who received nearly $1 trillion of your hard-earned tax dollars, only, in some cases, to have the audacity to turn around and ask for more? Some companies have continued to pay out huge bonuses. AIG alone paid out $530 million in bonuses, not to mention continuing to give lavish parties at sixteen-hundred-dollar-a-night hotels.

A funny thought occurred to me: Throughout this incredible chain of events, during which the American people watched their money go from Main Street to Wall Street, no one in Congress, no one in either the Bush Administration or the Obama Administration, and no one on Wall Street ever took time out to hold a news conference or place an advertisement on television, radio, or the Internet to say "thank you" to the American people. So I understand why so many Americans are angry, sad, and just plain tired of putting their trust in their government leaders. But please bear with me as I offer another insight into our present-day American psyche.

While we can shout it from the rooftops that we're mad as hell and we're not going to take it anymore, let us not forget something very fundamental. While we are pointing an accusing finger at all of the usual suspects and shouting, "Throw the bums out," let us not forget to examine the man or woman in the mirror. That's right; you and I are also to blame for the malaise we are currently experiencing. The trouble we are in is a shared responsibility. We the people helped bring ourselves to the brink of financial ruin, just as much as the leaders at the top. Take a little time out and look at yourself, and you will understand better the trouble the world is in.

We the people are the cause of the trouble in our housing market. If we had backed away from that adjustable rate mortgage, no matter how tempting it seemed, we might have avoided the eventual foreclosure because of the ballooning payments—payments that were way beyond our means. If we'd had the forethought and determination to downsize our dreams and buy a house within our means, we could have avoided the pain of losing our homes or going through such high anxiety each month when our mortgage payment came due.

The same principle applies to our spending habits with credit cards. How often have we seen something in the store and, because we had a credit card in our wallet or purse, purchased the product? There was a time when sound financial judgment would have overruled such impulses, and we would have waited until we had saved enough cash and then purchased the item of desire. By buying on credit, we indebt ourselves to credit card companies with high interest rates, getting ourselves in a never-ending cycle of monthly payments to the credit card company and finding ourselves frustrated because it seems that the principal never comes down. More bills equal more anxiety, and more anxiety equals a greater sense of failure.

While we are pointing an accusing finger at all of the usual suspects and shouting, "Throw the bums out," let us not forget to examine the man or woman in the mirror. That's right; you and I are also to blame for the malaise we are currently experiencing.

This merry-go-round of financial indiscretion can really ruin your marriage and undermine your relationship with your children. You find yourself always on edge, always agitated over the slightest difficulty that normally would not or should not concern you. But when you find yourself under duress from financial obligations you cannot meet, you become outraged over the most trivial things. This type of economic pain can even lead to divorce from your spouse and estrangement from your children. Then your American dream becomes a nightmare.

When you are stressed because of financial burdens, your children feel the pain. They sense what you are going through and, in their own way, they try to process the situation. But our children are not mentally or emotionally capable of shouldering adult problems in their preschool, elementary school, preteen or teenage years. Because of that, they often choose actions that are unhealthy. They may suffer poor grades in school, they may reach out to the wrong crowd of kids, getting involved in dangerous and risky behaviors (such as drug use, premarital sex, and/or gangs), or they may become totally withdrawn—alienating themselves from you and everyone else.

A proverb from the country of Ghana says: "The ruin of a nation begins in the homes of its people." To further explain this concept, allow me to use an analogy that Dr. Tony Evans, pastor of Oak Cliff Bible Fellowship in Dallas, Texas, so eloquently employs. If you have a "messed-up" parent raising a child, chances are good that you're going to have a "messed-up" child. Now if that "messed-up" child from that "messed-up" parent goes to school, you've got a "messed-up" school. If that "messed-up" child and/or that "messed-up" parent goes to church, you've got a "messed-up" church. Because that "messed-up" church, that "messed-up" school, and that "messed-up" child from that "messed-up" parent reside in a city, you've got a "messed-up" city. Because that "messed-up" city, that "messed-up" school, that "messed-up" church, and that "messed-up" child from that "messed-up parent" are located in a state, you've got a "messed-up" state. Because that "messed-up" state, city, church, school, and that "messed-up" child from that "messed-up" parent are part of a nation, you've got a "messed-up" nation. And since that "messed-up" nation is in the world, then it follows that you've got a "messed-up" world.

Right now, take a moment and take stock of the world we live in today. What do you see? Isn't it a mess? The sad reality about this "mess" we have created is that no one seems to know how to clean it up. Consider the facts: The President, the Congress, and Wall Street are trying to clean up the financial mess, and yet it seems as if we're stuck in quicksand. The more we try to move out of the mess, the deeper we sink. Unemployment is on the rise, and we are all concerned about job security. Who will be next to lose their job? Furthermore, how will we clean up the mess created by unemployment? The mess we are in is widespread. It's messy in government, messy in the private sector, messy globally, and certainly messy in our homes. So how do we clean it all up?

Government proposes more economic stimulus packages, but these are only temporary solutions to long-term problems. And what about you? How do you begin to clean up the mess in your home? How do you bridge the divide that exists between you and your spouse and you and your children? If you're divorced, it's only more complicated. How do you clean up the mess that plagues you and your ex-spouse and you and your children?

> *How do you bridge the divide that exists between you and your spouse and you and your children? If you're divorced, it's only more complicated. How do you clean up the mess that plagues you and your ex-spouse and you and your children?*

The story is told of a father who was working busily at home on a project for his job. As he studied and prepared, his six-year-old son was playing with toys and making a lot of noise in the adjacent room. Eventually, it became such a huge distraction that the father decided to find some project that would keep his son busy the rest of the day. He remembered that he had a puzzle of the world, so he assigned his son the task of putting that puzzle together. The son eagerly accepted the challenge, and the father returned to his work.

All was quiet for a while, and he could now focus on getting his project done, but then, only twenty minutes later, the son came bursting into the room, shouting with glee, "Daddy! Daddy! I finished the puzzle! It's great!" Amazed and bewildered that his son could complete such a complicated puzzle so quickly, the man followed the child into the room, wondering what he would find. To his surprise, the puzzle of the world had been completed to perfection. Every geographical location was in place.

The father scratched his head, looked at his son, and said, "You did a great job! But I'm curious; how did you finish it so quickly?" The son eagerly replied, "Oh, it was easy, Dad. On the back of the puzzle is the photo of a man. I put the man together, and the world just fell into place."

That was a "wow" moment for one proud dad, and it should be a "wow" moment for you and me too. If we learn anything from this father-and-son story, it should be this: If we can get man back together, then the world will come together.

But man cannot put himself back together. If you have lived long enough, you may have tried your level best to put your life together, but there is always something within your personality that makes you fall short of your goal to perfect yourself. Faced with today's crazy pop culture, you may be looking at yourself in the mirror and saying, "I'm not pretty enough." "I'm not handsome enough." "I'm too big." "I'm too fat." "I'm too poor." "I'm this" or "I'm that." Stop it! God loves you just the way you are.

In my years of living here on planet earth and traveling to foreign lands, I have learned of one common denominator between all members of the human race: we are not perfect and never will be perfect. As hard as we might try, we are prone to imperfection.

In the Geneva Study Bible of 1599, Psalm 8:4 reads: *"Lord, what is man, that thou takest knowledge of him? Or the son of man, that thou makest account of him?"* The commentary that follows explains:

> To give to God just praise, is to confess ourselves to be unworthy of so excellent benefits, and that He bestows them on us of His free mercy.
>
> Famed English clergyman Matthew Henry offers a more defined commentary on why man is important to God:
>
> 8:4: When men become eminent for things as to which they have had few advantages, they should be more deeply sensible that God has been their Teacher. Happy are those to whom the Lord gives that noblest victory, conquest and dominion over their own spirits. A prayer for further mercy is fitly begun with a thanksgiving for former mercy. There was a special power of God, inclining the people of Israel to be subject to David; it was typical of the bringing souls into subjection to the Lord Jesus. Man's days have little substance, considering how many

thoughts and cares of a never-dying soul are employed about a poor dying body. Man's life is as a shadow that passes away. In their highest earthly exaltation, believers will recollect how mean, sinful, and vile they are in themselves; thus they will be preserved from self-importance and presumption. God's time to help his people is when they are sinking and all other helps fail.

How fitting a time for Henry's commentary. He died in 1714, but the English clergyman zeroed in on where we are today in America and in the world. We find ourselves sinking, and all other attempts we make to help ourselves are failing. That's when God can step in, perhaps because we are no longer blinded by our own conceit and self-indulgence, in believing that we are the masters of our own destiny.

We must come to the conclusion that we are more than just flesh and blood, that we are also spirit. While we continue to make a mess of the flesh (the material world that we live in), let us not abandon the life-changing force of God working in us. It is the only way we can truly find transparency and transformation in our quest to improve our homes, our nation, and our world.

No man is an island. We must rely on God to change our hearts, cause us to forge a new outlook and attitude within us, and give us fresh thinking, new ideas that will deliver us from our own disastrous decisions. Our present conditions were not caused by God but by our own foolish choices. Now is the time to establish a holy alliance with our Sovereign Maker. In this manner, I believe we can set a course for achieving the impossible, for our Lord Jesus Christ has said: *"The things which are impossible with men are possible with God"* (Luke 18:27).

Indeed, we have before us an impossible task, to turn our economy around, to responsibly end two wars, to win the war on terror, to build a greater understanding globally, to prepare a better future for our children, to overcome defeat against all odds.

This is not a time for the feeble of heart. America and the world need strong and courageous people of faith. Let this serve as a notice to agnostics and atheists. I understand and respect your wishes, to believe that you can make it without God, but I submit this statement from one of today's most successful musical performers and songwriters in my defense of God:

> Ninety-three million miles from the blistering surface of the sun hangs the planet earth, a rotating sphere perfectly suspended in the center of the universe, the ultimate creation from an infinite mind, an unbelievably intricate complex design, a supernatural testimony, an irrefutable sign that there is a God.
>
> The size, position, and angle of the earth is a scientific phenomenon to see. A few degrees closer

to the sun and we'd disintegrate, a few degrees further away, we'd freeze. The axis of the earth is tilted at a perfect twenty-three-degree angle, and it's no mistake that it is. This allows equal global distribution of the rays of the sun, making it possible for the food chain to exist.

Or take, for example, the combination of nitrogen and oxygen in the atmosphere we breathe every day. It just happens to be the exact mix that life needs to prosper. It doesn't happen on any other planet that way.

You see, the Bible says the invisible things of God are seen through His creation. To believe this is not hard. If there's a design, there's a Designer, if there's a plan, there's a Planner, and if there's a miracle, there is a God.

The Scripture says, *"the heavens declare the glory of God and the skies proclaim the work of His hands."* If we

Indeed we have before us an impossible task, to turn our economy around, to responsibly end two wars, to win the war on terror, to build a greater understanding globally, to prepare a better future for our children, to overcome defeat against all odds.

allowed our minds to drink in all the truth that surrounds us, creation itself would help us understand. Did you know the moon controls the tides. It's the maid that cleans the oceans. Even the waves don't crash the shores in vain. The tides drag impurities from the depths of the sea. This is nature's constant recycling chain.

It simply boggles the mind to think that the stars will rotate with such exact precision, but it's true. The atomic clock, with an error factor of less than three seconds per millennium, is set by the way they move; though they silently orbit, the sun, the moon, and the stars, like celestial evangelists above, circle the earth every twenty-four hours shouting in every language that there is a God.

Atheism is the wedge under the foundation of our faith, trying to topple our relationship with Christ. When the fool says in his heart, *"There is no God,"* he rejects the truth God painted on the canvas of the night. Atheism has never created an artistic masterpiece, never healed a fatal disease or calmed a fear. Atheism has never given answers to our existence, peace to a troubled mind, or even dried a tear.

For it's God who created heaven and earth and flung the stars into space and breathed into a handful of dirt, and it became a man. It's God who sits on the circle of the earth and measures the mountains in a scale, and holds the seven seas in the palm of His hand. It's God who sent His only begotten Son to the cross of Calvary to save our souls from hell and the grave. It's God who creates, God who delivers, God who heals, and God who is worthy of a thunderous ovation of praise.

There is a hope, there is a light.

There is an answer to all answers.

There is a flame that burns in the night.

And I know, I know, I know there is a God.

— *Carman, from the album R.I.O.T.*
(Righteous Invasion of Truth)

If we can come to the end of ourselves and accept God's plan for our lives, we can change the person we see in the mirror. We can see ourselves transformed from what we once were into a child of God, entitled to all the blessings that He bestows upon us.

"Righteousness, peace, and joy in the Holy Ghost" (Romans 14:17, in the King James Version of the Bible), … how similar that sounds to "life, liberty, and the pursuit of happiness." If we surrender our will to God's perfect will, I believe we will learn to debate and even disagree on all matters pertaining to our lives and yet, through prayer, find the common ground that will help us to improve the village that helps raise our children.

America's Hope

With God's help and guidance, through Jesus Christ, we can create a beloved community, taking our "mess" and turning it into a message, and then becoming messengers of hope. Let faith, hope, and love flood our homes, spilling over into our nation. While the proverb from Ghana says, "The ruin of a nation begins in the homes of its people," I believe the converse to be true as well. The greatness of a nation begins in the homes of its people. So, dear friend, let us take our stand for God, for our families, for our nation, and for the world. Let your home be where greatness begins. And pass it on!

This, my friends, is *America's Hope*.

Chapter Eight

Repairing the Broken Foundations

Take a look around. Walk the streets of America. What do you see? Do you see homeless people still begging for money, still flashing cardboard signs that read "Will work for food?" Where is the church?

I know what it feels like to be homeless. I've experienced it. I shall never forget how it all came about. I was working as a news reporter for WJCL-TV in Savannah, Georgia. The pay was terribly low, which made it extremely difficult to support a wife and baby daughter. So in my attempt to make ends meet, I started moonlighting as a lounge singer at the lovely Courtyard by Mariott hotel on Hilton Head Island.

My first wife and I were already undergoing some intense struggles that threatened our fragile marriage, and adding to our marital woes was a mountain of debt that continued to climb. These latest financial troubles quickly exacerbated the situation, and like a pressure-cooker that was functioning improperly, our angry, sad, and bitter emotions boiled over, spewing out the broken pieces of our marriage, overflowing into a subsequent separation and eventual divorce.

I quickly learned the meaning of the old saying "When it rains, it pours." Living on my own, I sought to get my life together, but I was fired after a story appeared in the Sunday edition of the *Savannah News and Evening Press*. It erroneously reported that I was temporarily leaving my job at WJCL to pursue a career in professional singing. My bosses read the article and went ballistic, firing me on the spot, unwilling to hear my repeated protests that the article was false.

With no place to stay, no one to turn to, and nowhere to go (because I didn't have money to go anywhere), I began living out of my car.

Shortly after that, I moved to Atlanta, hoping to secure a new job as a news reporter at one of the local stations there, but the response was not good. No Atlanta station was willing to hire me. After staying with friends for two weeks, I decided I had better move out before I had overstayed my welcome.

Now, with no place to stay, no one to turn to, and nowhere to go (because I didn't have money to go anywhere), I began living out of my car. I found a job peddling imitation leather goods on the streets of Atlanta, shifting from street corner to street corner and from mall parking lot to mall parking lot, desperately seeking someone who would listen to my sales pitch and buy a handbag, suitcase, or briefcase for under fifty dollars. The experience was humiliating. From TV news reporter to peddler. It's a subject for another book, but the point is that I have experienced homelessness, living out of my car and sleeping in a warehouse (hesitant to go to a homeless shelter because I was fearful that someone would steal my last remaining possessions). The experience remains indelibly etched in my memory, and I wrote about it in a song I recorded several years ago to highlight the plight of the homeless:

> *Homeless people living on the street, crying for some help, but we don't see their need.*
> *We pass by them like we don't even care, too busy with our own lives to lend a hand to share.*
> *Now what are we gonna do? After all, it could be me or you.*
> *Take away our jobs and our money; and we could be homeless too.*
> *C'mon, get on up, get into, please. Let's get involved.*
> *Put our faith in Jesus, and we can get this problem solved.*

It could have been you or me.
Seek the truth, the way, the light.
It could have been you or me.
Come to Christ; He'll make it right.

Little baby cries himself to sleep.
His mommy sells her body to get him food to eat.
She's left with nowhere to turn because Daddy isn't
*   there.*
And we don't have the time to let her know we care.
We're too busy to pray with the preacher.
And we are too busy to learn from the teacher.
C'mon, please make a change before it's too late.
Lend a helping hand. Please don't hesitate.
It could have been you or me.
Seek the truth, the way, the light.
It could have been you or me.
Come to Christ; He'll make it right.

Jesus says to us, "Were your there when I was home-
*   less? Did you help Me find some shelter?*
Were you there when I was down and out? Did you
*   save Me from disaster?*
Were you there when I was hungry? Did you feed
*   Me from your table?*
Were you there when I was naked? Did you clothe
*   Me? I know you were able."*
— MESSAGE TO AMERICA by Kelly Wright

Repairing the Broken Foundations

Oh, America, why have we strayed from our first love: loving God with all our heart and soul? Didn't Jesus say, *"Inasmuch as you did it to one of the least of these My brethren, you did it to Me"* (Matthew 25:40)? Wake up, America! Wake up!

The famed researcher George Barna conducted a study several years ago and discovered that if every church in America would make the effort to take in five homeless families, feed them, clothe them, nurture them, and help them get back on their feet, it would eradicate poverty in America. Look at what God said through Isaiah:

> *"Shout it aloud, do not hold back.*
> *Raise your voice like a trumpet.*
> *Declare to my people their rebellion and to the house of Jacob their sins.*
> *For day after day they seek me out; they seem eager to know my ways,*
> *as if they were a nation that does what is right and has not forsaken the commands of its God.*
> *They ask me for just decisions and seem eager for God to come near them.*
> *'Why have we fasted,' they say, 'and you have not seen it?*
> *Why have we humbled ourselves, and you have not noticed?'*
>
> *"Yet on the day of your fasting, you do as you please and exploit all your workers.*

*Your fasting ends in quarreling and strife, and in
striking each other with wicked fists.
You cannot fast as you do today and expect your
voice to be heard on high."*

Isaiah 58:1-4, NIV

This message from the book of Isaiah was written centuries ago. It was a direct word from God spoken to the Jewish people through the prophet. At the time of this significant dialogue between God and man, the Lord was concerned about Israel's lack of faith, loss of purpose, and faintness of heart in trusting Him to deliver them from their enemies.

In fact, the greatest enemy they faced was themselves. Instead of being a humble people, grateful for the bounty that God had bestowed upon them, they became a nation of grumbling, complaining, murmuring, gossiping, and sniping individuals. Ungrateful, unloving, and unholy, they filled their hearts with a false sense of entitlement. They reasoned that because they were God's chosen people, they could do no wrong. All they had to do was snap their fingers and make their demands, and God would provide.

In His straightforward address to them in this passage, God sets the record straight, much as He is doing with America today. For we, too, have become a calloused, cynical, obstinate, and stiff-necked people, refusing to humble ourselves before a loving God and pray for help in our times of need and trouble.

Repairing the Broken Foundations

Consider how much quarreling and strife goes on among us. Consider how some of our young people are caught up in the gang-life, where violence is the norm, so that they strike each other with wicked fists or, worse, shoot each other without giving it a second thought.

One other point of clarification here, lest you are tempted to say, "This does not apply to me." God is talking to His people in this passage, and today, in this time, *we* are His people, so He is speaking to the church, to those who acknowledge Him as the Creator of the world. It is the church that knows the significance of fasting, and yet God is saying that our programs and agendas will never produce any good fruit if we are not conducting ourselves in a spirit of trusting Him with all that we have. He goes on to say:

At the time of this significant dialogue between God and man, the Lord was concerned about Israel's lack of faith, loss of purpose, and faintness of heart in trusting Him to deliver them from their enemies. In fact, the greatest enemy they faced was themselves.

"Is this the kind of fast I have chosen, only a day for a man to humble himself?

Is it only for bowing one's head like a reed and for
lying on sackcloth and ashes?
Is that what you call a fast, a day acceptable to the
LORD ?

Is not this the kind of fasting I have chosen: to loose
the chains of injustice and untie the cords of the
yoke, to set the oppressed free and break every
yoke?
Is it not to share your food with the hungry and to
provide the poor wanderer with shelter—when
you see the naked, to clothe him, and not to turn
away from your own flesh and blood?"

Isaiah 58:5-7, NIV

We somehow expect government to step in and remedy all of America's social ills. How quickly we have forgotten the initiative that President George W. Bush launched in his first term to help end these kinds of societal problems. He called it the Faith-Based and Community Initiative, and it was a bold endeavor to get the faith community to partner with government and the private sector to address the incredible needs that have kept many Americans on the bottom rung of the ladder, trapped in poverty and despair.

President Bush signed the Faith-Based and Community Initiative as an executive order on January 21, 2001, but after the attacks of 9/11 and the subsequent start of war in Iraq and Afghanistan, news about the program faded from the headlines. The needs, however, were still very pressing throughout the country's rural and urban areas. President Barack Obama has vowed to keep the program running. During his presidential campaign, he explained to a group of evangelicals at the Eastside Community Ministry in Zanesville, Ohio:

> The challenges we face today ... are simply too big for government to solve alone. We need all hands on deck.

In January 2008, President Bush addressed a faith-based group that was helping the families of persons who were incarcerated, plus offering aid to the men and women upon their release from prison. Baltimore, Maryland's Jericho Program would not be a success were it not for people getting over their political differences, relying on their faith, and working with the President's program to reach out and touch a part of their community in need.

FROM THE OFFICE OF THE WHITE HOUSE
President Bush Discusses the Faith-Based and Community Initiative Jericho Program

Baltimore, Maryland Fact Sheet: The Faith-Based and Community Initiative: A Quiet Revolution in the Way Government Addresses Human Need

My administration created the White House Office of Faith-Based and Community Initiatives to deal with this problem. We wanted to focus our government and taxpayers' money on solutions, on effective programs, and we recognized that many of the effective programs existed in the faith community. Washington, D.C., oftentimes is a process-oriented town. We need to work hard to make it a results-oriented town. And if one of the compelling national interests is to help good people who have been in prison come back and readjust, and learn skills and attitudes necessary to be a productive citizen, if that's an important national concern, then we ought to turn to programs that are meeting those results. That's what we ought to do.

There are programs to help provide mentors for 70,000

> *Baltimore, Maryland's Jericho Program would not be a success were it not for people getting over their political differences, relying on their faith, and working with the President's program to reach out and touch a part of their community in need.*

children whose parents are incarcerated. There are programs to help deal with drug addiction and alcohol addiction, programs to help young people in our inner cities escape gangs. These are all programs where a faith-based or community group has dedicated their lives to solve a problem. And it makes sense for the federal government to give these programs a chance to access taxpayers' money. – January 2008

The release went on to explain more about the program and the fruit it was bearing:

The Initiative is changing the way government addresses human need by making grants, programs, and other opportunities more accessible to new faith-based and community partners. For example, through initiatives such as the voucher-based Access to Recovery Program, the Administration is working to expand individual choice so that Americans in need of substance-abuse treatment and recovery support services can receive help from the program that best suits them. In addition, the Compassion Capital Fund, another signature program of the Initiative, is helping small grassroots organizations that have never received federal funding build the capacity they need to compete for federal grants and serve their communities.

The Initiative is producing real results for people in need. For example:

Prisoner Reentry Initiative: Released inmates who participate in the Prisoner Reentry Initiative, which links adult nonviolent offenders who are reentering society with FBCOs based in the cities to which they return, are returning to prison at less than half the national rate.

Mentoring Children of Prisoners: More than 70,000 children whose parents are behind bars have been matched with caring mentors under the Mentoring Children of Prisoners program, which is on-track to reach its goal of 100,000 matches this year.

President's Emergency Plan for AIDS Relief: The President's Emergency Plan for AIDS Relief (PEPFAR) represents massive-scale implementation of the Initiative's vision. In the PEPFAR's 15 focus countries, more than 80 percent of PEPFAR partners are indigenous organizations, and more than 20 percent of all partners are faith-based.

Repairing the Broken Foundations

Under the Faith-Based and Community Initiative, federal agencies have built on the success of Charitable Choice by issuing Equal Treatment regulations to level the playing field for faith-based organizations across a much broader array of programs. An audit conducted after the Faith-Based and Community Initiative was launched in 2001 confirmed the federal government was often suspicious of faith-based organizations and excluded these groups altogether from certain programs or burdened them with excessive, unnecessary regulations. The Equal Treatment regulations clarify faith-based organizations' eligibility to participate in federal social service programs on the same basis as any other private organization, and provide clear and detailed guidance regarding faith-based organizations' rights and responsibilities regarding religious character, independence, and religious activities.

Thirty-five governors—19 Democrats and 16 Republicans—and more than 100 mayors have offices or liaisons dedicated to strengthening faith-based and community organizations and extending their vital works. Twelve of these states have changed governors, some across party lines, but not one has ended their efforts.

As a nation, under President Bush's guidance, we have given more than $30 billion to the Faith-Based Initiative to fight AIDS and malaria in Africa. To date, President Bush has done more than any other world leader to deal with the pandemic spread of AIDS in Africa. What he did required bold leadership, purpose, and an abiding faith in God to follow what Jesus discusses in Matthew 25:40. Again, He said: *"Inasmuch as you did it to one of the least of these My brethren, you did it to Me."* While two wars and a beleaguered economy have maligned the reputation of President George W. Bush, I applaud him for his visionary leadership to look beyond the political divide and lead the nation in the fight to help those in need. I pray that President Barack Obama, who says he is driven by the same faith in Jesus Christ as his predecessor was, will boldly continue as indicated in a White House press release following his signing of an executive order:

The White House, Washington (February 5, 2009)

President Barack Obama today signed an executive order establishing the new White House Office of Faith-Based and Neighborhood Partnerships. The White House Office of Faith-Based and Neighborhood Partnerships will work on behalf of Americans committed to improving their communities, no matter their religious or political beliefs.

Repairing the Broken Foundations

Over the past few days and weeks, there has been much talk about what our government's role should be during this period of economic emergency. That is as it should be, because there is much that government can and must do to help people in need. But no matter how much money we invest or how sensibly we design our policies, the change that Americans are looking for will not come from government alone. There is a force for good greater than government. It is an expression of faith, this yearning to give back, this hungering for a purpose larger than our own, that reveals itself not simply in places of worship, but in senior centers and shelters, schools and hospitals, and any place an American decides.

This Faith-Based and Neighborhood Partnerships is one area of

> *As a nation, under President Bush's guidance, we have given more than $30 billion to the Faith-Based Initiative to fight AIDS and malaria in Africa. To date, President Bush has done more than any other world leader to deal with the pandemic spread of AIDS in Africa.*

government that breaks down the political divide. Liberals and Conservatives, Republicans and Democrats, can work together, sharing their faith, talents, and gifts to help "the least of these." Just as the popular "God" billboard campaign says, "The benefits are out of this world."

Consider the advice that God provides us through the prophet Isaiah. As noted earlier in the chapter, in Isaiah 58, God addresses the people of Israel about conducting their lives as leaders who reach out to help people in need, to touch their lives with the kind of benevolence and care that leads to a productive and successful life. The people of Israel were on a fast, but they began questioning God when their fasting failed to produce the desired results. They wanted immediate gratification from their fast—prosperity and the good life. But God questioned their motives for the fast and observed their shortcomings in displaying their love for Him and those who stood in need of help. It is a behavior that many people living today have adopted, following their own way instead of relying on God to lead them.

Jesus also addresses the issue:

> *"Then the King will say to those on his right, 'Enter, you who are blessed by my Father! Take what's coming to you in this kingdom. It's been ready for you since the world's foundation. And here's why:*
>
> *I was hungry and you fed me,*
> *I was thirsty and you gave me a drink,*

Repairing the Broken Foundations

I was homeless and you gave me a room,
I was shivering and you gave me clothes,
I was sick and you stopped to visit,
I was in prison and you came to me.'

"Then those 'sheep' are going to say, 'Master, what
are you talking about? When did we ever see you
hungry and feed you, thirsty and give you a drink?
And when did we ever see you sick or in prison and
come to you?' Then the King will say, 'I'm telling
the solemn truth: Whenever you did one of these
things to someone overlooked or ignored, that was
me—you did it to me.'
"Then he will turn to the 'goats,' the ones on his left,
and say, 'Get out, worthless goats! You're good for
nothing but the fires of hell. And why? Because—

I was hungry and you gave me no meal,
I was thirsty and you gave me no drink,
I was homeless and you gave me no bed,
I was shivering and you gave me no clothes,
Sick and in prison, and you never visited.'

"Then those 'goats' are going to say, 'Master, what
are you talking about? When did we ever see you
hungry or thirsty or homeless or shivering or sick or
in prison and didn't help?'

"He will answer them, 'I'm telling the solemn truth: Whenever you failed to do one of these things to someone who was being overlooked or ignored, that was me—you failed to do it to me.'"

Matthew 25:34-45, MSG

> *If we could learn to apply biblical principles to our worldly problems, we could repair the broken foundations of our country and even of the world.*

Jesus was concerned about *"the least of these."* Certainly, from this passage of Scripture, one can see how the plan that God offers could apply to all areas of our lives—our troubled economy, the housing market, health care, and our energy woes. If we could learn to apply biblical principles to our worldly problems, we could repair the broken foundations of our country and even of the world.

I know, for some of you who are reading this, all of this talk about our place in the world through God is hard to fathom. You're probably approaching it with a degree of cynicism and skepticism. You reason to yourself, "Anyone can take Scripture and twist and use it to support their own argument." And that would be true. Many people do manipulate the Bible for their own selfish ends. But consider the focus of my message. It is not about me, and it is not about you; it is about God and about us as a people making full use of our faith in God to live a life that's full, a life that enables us to touch the world by meeting people at their point of need.

Surely, I could spend a lot of time writing a message of doom and gloom, but my sole desire is to provide you with promises from God that His plans for us are not meant for disaster but for a future and a hope. There are skeptics and cynics who would love to keep people in fear and confusion. I write and share God's Word with the desire of letting you know that with God we have no need to fear, for *"God has not given us a spirit of fear, but of power and of love and of a sound mind"* (2 Timothy 1:7). It is that spiritual power that we must harness, and that sound mind that we must develop, using them both to develop strategies that will restore our land in the midst of crime, sickness, poverty, unemployment, confusion, and doubt.

The apostle Paul was no stranger to perilous times. His faith, hope, and love for Jesus Christ sustained him through persecution, imprisonment, triumph, and trials, and even when he was facing certain death. Paul always found a reason to celebrate his life with God, and therefore his life is an example of how living by faith can make all of us overcomers against all odds. Paul constantly sought to encourage people, urging them to always rejoice and not to be anxious or worried about anything:

Celebrate God all day, every day. I mean, revel in him! Make it as clear as you can to all you meet that you're on their side, working with them and not against them. Help them see that the Master is about to arrive. He could show up any minute!

Don't fret or worry. Instead of worrying, pray. Let petitions and praises shape your worries into prayers, letting God know your concerns. Before you know it, a sense of God's wholeness, everything coming together for good, will come and settle you down. It's wonderful what happens when Christ displaces worry at the center of your life.

Summing it all up, friends, I'd say you'll do best by filling your minds and meditating on things true, noble, reputable, authentic, compelling, gracious—the best, not the worst; the beautiful, not the ugly; things to praise, not things to curse. Put into practice what you learned from me, what you heard and saw and realized. Do that, and God, who makes everything work together, will work you into his most excellent harmonies.

Philippians 4:4-9, MSG

We must be willing to exercise our faith in God's Word. That's the only way we can find a lamp for our feet and light for our path that will lead us out of the collective darkness that is creating a blinding fog in every area of our lives—politics, economics, government, home, and even faith. If we can forge ahead, adopting God's principles, we can learn to tear down the walls of hate, bitterness, envy, and doubt that divide us and keep us ensnared in doom and gloom without a future and a hope:

> *It wasn't so long ago that you were mired in that old stagnant life of sin. You let the world, which doesn't know the first thing about living, tell you how to live. You filled your lungs with polluted unbelief, and then exhaled disobedience. We all did it, all of us doing what we felt like doing, when we felt like doing it, all of us in the same boat. It's a wonder God didn't lose his temper and do away with the whole lot of us. Instead, immense in mercy and with an incredible love, he embraced us. He took our sin-dead lives and made us alive in Christ. He did all this on his own, with no help from us! Then he picked us up and set us down in highest heaven in company with Jesus, our Messiah.*
>
> Ephesians 2:1-6, MSG

With faith, hope, and love, we can reach across our political partisan divide, we can reach out beyond the color of our skin, we can reach out and touch the hearts of men, women, and children who are trying to escape "messed up" lives.

This, my friends, is *America's Hope.*

Chapter Nine

Out of the Wilderness

I watched the news today, and I had to turn my head away.

Troubles everywhere ... I see a world filled with great despair.

Mothers crying, children dying, soldiers fighting, politicians always lying.

Somebody tell me why. Why can't we live together?

Why can't we get along? Why do we hurt each other, making each other cry?

Why can't we right what's wrong? Why can't we get along?

— WHY by Kelly Wright

Take a good look around. What do you see? Trouble is forcing its way into the lives of men, women, and children. From every village to every hamlet, every rural community to every urban area, there is trouble with a capital "T."

Poverty, hunger, homelessness, and violence seep through the splendor of our cities that boast modern-day conveniences but can't find a way to cure their societal ills. In developing countries, governments are powerless to stop the spread of famine, starvation, HIV-AIDs and malaria. These painful realities confront us every day.

How do we navigate our way through this meandering mess, this worldwide web of recklessness and wanton neglect of each other? Is there a remedy for our dilemma?

At the risk of overstating this fact, I want to state it once again: Our elected leaders continue to govern from a partisan divide. I believe some of the incentive to continue this partisan sniping comes from the very people who elected them to office. Many of *us* cling to deep-seated beliefs that keep us from reaching out to each other. We live in our own little enclaves of ideology, political allegiance, and racial or ethnic identity, and many of us refuse to enjoy being part of the American melting pot with its delightful and flavorful stew called Americana.

God, who created us, knows us, and therefore He understands us. Our modern-day town criers are the talk-show hosts of radio and television, and the bloggers of the Webosphere. They are the mouthpieces who express the partisanship. Those who speak to our culture must stand up and forge the new common ground. But talk-show hosts from both sides of the spectrum continue to bombard the American people with talk about who's right and who's wrong, who's on the Left and who's on the Right? I say, "Enough is enough!"

My message to all of the modern-day town criers, the talk-show hosts on the Right and on the Left, is this: First, I applaud your talent and oratory skills. You are exceptional at what you do, and you have earned a very rewarding lifestyle from your abilities. But may I suggest that you try talking to people from a godly point of view instead of from the point of view of Right-wing or Left-wing politics.

> I believe some of the incentive to continue this partisan sniping comes from the very people who elected them to office. Many of us cling to deep-seated beliefs that keep us from reaching out to each other.

Please consider this: Over the centuries, God used many men and women as His mouthpieces, to speak for Him. They bore the distinction of being called *prophets*. Their lives were steeped in faith, even though they were sometimes caught in fearful situations. They were rich in love and powerful in God's divine wisdom, and so He spoke to them and through them to the masses.

Please consider the influence God blesses you with each day. Before you sit down at the microphone, be sure your brain is engaged before you put your mouth in gear. Let's go one step further and deeper: Be sure your heart is filled with the Word of God so that when you speak, what proceeds out of your mouth will come from the heart of God. From this moment forward, may you come to know that the transformation of America and the world you long for can only come through the power of God. He said, *"And do not be conformed to this world, but be transformed by the renewing of your mind, that you may prove what is that good and acceptable and perfect will of God"* (Romans 12:2). It might be helpful to look at the entire passage:

> *So here's what I want you to do, God helping you: Take your everyday, ordinary life—your sleeping, eating, going-to-work, and walking-around life—and place it before God as an offering. Embracing what God does for you is the best thing you can do for him. Don't become so well-adjusted to your culture that you fit into it without even thinking. Instead, fix your attention on God. You'll be changed from the inside out. Readily recognize what he wants from you, and quickly respond to it. Unlike the culture around you, always dragging you down to its level of immaturity, God brings the best out of you, develops well-formed maturity in you.*
>
> *I'm speaking to you out of deep gratitude for all that God has given me, and especially as I have responsi-*

bilities in relation to you. Living then, as every one of you does, in pure grace, it's important that you not misinterpret yourselves as people who are bringing this goodness to God. No, God brings it all to you. The only accurate way to understand ourselves is by what God is and by what he does for us, not by what we are and what we do for him.

Romans 12:1-3, MSG

Dear talk-show friends (who hold so much sway over the populace), I pray that you consider it wise to speak words of life, wisdom, and encouragement into the lives of your listeners and your viewers. All of you have the ability to make a bold statement to the nation and to the world by speaking to the soul of America, which is not Conservative, Liberal, or Independent—but American. After all, God is above politics and religion. Therefore, I encourage you to speak boldly the truth about how God sees the world as it is today. Consider what Jesus said about the times in which we currently live:

One day people were standing around talking about the Temple, remarking how beautiful it was, the splendor of its stonework and memorial gifts. Jesus said, "All this you're admiring so much—the time is coming when every stone in that building will end up in a heap of rubble."

They asked him, "Teacher, when is this going to

happen? What clue will we get that it's about to take place?"

He said, *"Watch out for the doomsday deceivers. Many leaders are going to show up with forged identities claiming, 'I'm the One,' or, 'The end is near.' Don't fall for any of that. When you hear of wars and uprisings, keep your head and don't panic. This is routine history and no sign of the end."*

He went on: *"Nation will fight nation and ruler fight ruler, over and over. Huge earthquakes will occur in various places. There will be famines. You'll think at times that the very sky is falling.*

"But before any of this happens, they'll arrest you, hunt you down, and drag you to court and jail. It will go from bad to worse, dog-eat-dog, everyone at your throat because you carry my name. You'll end up on the witness stand, called to testify. Make up your mind right now not to worry about it. I'll give you the

words and wisdom that will reduce all your accusers to stammers and stutters.

"You'll even be turned in by parents, brothers, relatives, and friends. Some of you will be killed. There's no telling who will hate you because of me. Even so, every detail of your body and soul—even the hairs of your head!—is in my care; nothing of you will be lost. Staying with it—that's what is required. Stay with it to the end. You won't be sorry; you'll be saved.

"When you see soldiers camped all around Jerusalem, then you'll know that she is about to be devastated. If you're living in Judea at the time, run for the hills. If you're in the city, get out quickly. If you're out in the fields, don't go home to get your coat. This is Vengeance Day—everything written about it will come to a head. Pregnant and nursing mothers will have it especially hard. Incredible misery! Torrential rage! People dropping like flies; people dragged off to prisons; Jerusalem under the boot of barbarians until the nations finish what was given them to do.

"It will seem like all hell has broken loose—sun, moon, stars, earth, sea, in an uproar and everyone all over the world in a panic, the wind knocked out of them by the threat of doom, the powers-that-be quaking.

"And then—then!—they'll see the Son of Man welcomed in grand style—a glorious welcome! When all this starts to happen, up on your feet. Stand tall with your heads high. Help is on the way!"

He told them a story. "Look at a fig tree. Any tree for that matter. When the leaves begin to show, one look tells you that summer is right around the corner. The same here—when you see these things happen, you know God's kingdom is about here. Don't brush this off: I'm not just saying this for some future generation, but for this one, too—these things will happen. Sky and earth will wear out; my words won't wear out.

"But be on your guard. Don't let the sharp edge of your expectation get dulled by parties and drinking and shopping. Otherwise, that Day is going to take you by complete surprise, spring on you suddenly like a trap, for it's going to come on everyone, everywhere, at once. So, whatever you do, don't go to sleep at the switch. Pray constantly that you will have the strength and wits to make it through everything that's coming and end up on your feet before the Son of Man."

He spent his days in the Temple teaching, but his nights out on the mountain called Olives. All the people were up at the crack of dawn to come to the Temple and listen to him.   Luke 21:5-38, MSG

Out of the Wilderness

Dear talk-show friends, if this message is too strong or too over-the-top and is too lacking in political correctness for your audiences, consider this more sedate, yet still penetrating, message of a dangerous unselfishness:

"God blesses those who are poor and realize their need for him,
for the Kingdom of Heaven is theirs.
God blesses those who mourn,
for they will be comforted.
God blesses those who are humble,
for they will inherit the whole earth.
God blesses those who hunger and thirst for justice,
for they will be satisfied.
God blesses those who are merciful,
for they will be shown mercy.
God blesses those whose hearts are pure,
for they will see God.
God blesses those who work for peace,
for they will be called the children of God.
God blesses those who are persecuted for doing right,
for the Kingdom of Heaven is theirs.

God blesses you when people mock you and persecute you and lie about you and say all sorts of evil things against you because you are my followers. Be happy about it! Be very glad! For a great reward awaits you in heaven. And remember, the ancient prophets were persecuted in the same way.

You are the salt of the earth. But what good is salt if it has lost its flavor? Can you make it salty again? It will be thrown out and trampled underfoot as worthless.

You are the light of the world—like a city on a hilltop that cannot be hidden. No one lights a lamp and then puts it under a basket. Instead, a lamp is placed on a stand, where it gives light to everyone in the house. In the same way, let your good deeds shine out for all to see, so that everyone will praise your heavenly Father."   Matthew 5:3-16, NLT

The powerful words of Jesus are penetrating. God's entire Word cuts deep into the heart of all humankind:

For the word of God is living and powerful, and sharper than any two-edged sword, piercing even to the division of soul and spirit, and of joints and marrow, and is a discerner of the thoughts and intents of the heart. And there is no creature hidden from His sight, but all things are naked and open to the eyes of Him to whom we must give account.
Hebrews 4:12-13

THE MESSAGE says it this way:

Out of the Wilderness

God means what he says. What he says goes. His powerful Word is sharp as a surgeon's scalpel, cutting through everything, whether doubt or defense, laying us open to listen and obey. Nothing and no one is impervious to God's Word. We can't get away from it—no matter what.

So, here we are ... Americans divided along ideological and political lines. We're divided on the wars in Iraq and Afghanistan, over how to deal with a crumbling economy, the mortgage crisis, health care, and much more. These divisions are unhealthy and give the lie to our being "one nation under God, indivisible, with liberty and justice for all." Yet, as we just read in the Scriptures, God's Word cuts through all of it. The question is: Are we willing to trust and obey Him? Or will we continue to follow our own way, which will only lead to more rancor and division?

In the pages of this book, I have

So, here we are ... Americans divided along political and ideological lines. We're divided on the wars in Iraq and Afghanistan, over how to deal with a crumbling economy, the mortgage crisis, health care, and much more.

been making my own personal observations about our society, which I believe has been experiencing much emotional, intellectual, and spiritual distress. Now I believe it's time for us to send out an SOS, a distress signal, to God Himself that we are in need of an emergency response. We are in desperate need of urgent care: resuscitation of the American heart, American mind, American soul. If we are not careful to overcome this dysfunction by following God's prescription for redemption, I suspect that we will descend into bitterness, frustration, and chaos. We have no no time to lose. As President Barack Obama said so often during his presidential campaign, "This is our moment; this is our time."

It is time that we believe and stand on God's Word to battle the forces of evil that seek to divide and conquer us. It is time that we forge ahead with a new commitment to moral clarity that will enable us to grasp the real essence of "love God and love your neighbor as yourself." It is time to realize that our politicians alone will not save us. We are in need of a Savior.

Let me be clear. I still believe the United States is a beacon of hope to the world. We are still a light that shines where the rest of the world is dim. But I pray that we will be empowered to shine that light even brighter, not allowing it to be dimmed because of our political infighting, nor allowing it to be extinguished because of our partisanship and prejudice.

Out of the Wilderness

I seek to awaken all of us to some of the ways I believe we can gain unity in our purpose. I am one who believes that whatever label you may wear—Black, White, yellow, red, or brown—if you believe in Jesus, you belong with me. And, in Jesus, even in the midst of despair, hope always prevails:

> *And not only that, but we also glory in tribulations, knowing that tribulation produces perseverance; and perseverance, character; and character, hope. Now hope does not disappoint, because the love of God has been poured out in our hearts by the Holy Spirit who was given to us.*
>
> Romans 5:3-5

Consider this, pray about it, adopt it into your life, and watch this nation flourish even in the worst of times. Embrace God and engage the world. Hold on to your American dream, but let that dream be rooted in God's Word.

Let us hold on to our American heritage, but let us cast off our petty pride and prejudices. Let us hold on to our common cause—to be a nation that reaches across boundaries and borders to help people in need everywhere. Let us together enter a Promised Land of faith, hope, and love. Let us govern ourselves with God's Word reigning supreme within our laws.

We have much work to do. Let us never lose sight of the clear and ever-present danger of idleness and fear, which will only divide us. Let us keep our eyes on God, knowing that He will help us overcome despair, for freedom is our cause and heaven is our destiny. We are one nation, and we must strive to remain under God, indivisible, with liberty and justice for all. We are trusting Him that there will be no diminishing of our destiny.

May God bless America. May God bless the world. Save us all. This is our prayer.

This, my friends, is *America's Hope*.

Chapter 10

A Time for Healing

No work is insignificant. All labor that uplifts humanity has dignity and importance and should be undertaken with painstaking excellence.
— Dr. Martin Luther King, Jr.

"Look, Daddy, there's a nigger!"

Those words stunned me. I was strolling through the aisles of the A&P supermarket in Hagerstown, Maryland, doing some shopping for my grandmother when I heard those ugly words ring out; and in this unpleasant way, my errand was suddenly and violently interrupted.

Taken aback, I looked down into a nearby supermarket cart to where the sound had come from, and there, sitting in the cart, was a child who could not have been more than four. He had been pointing his little finger toward me as he spoke those startling words to his father, who was standing nearby, and the finger was still pointing in my direction.

I was "blown away" by this, and my mind was sent racing with all sorts of thoughts. How could a child so young know such a dirty, despicable word? How? Why? What kind of "jerk" would teach such words to a baby? One gaze at the child's father gave me all the answer I needed. He never responded, but gave me a withering look and then turned away and continued his shopping as if nothing had happened.

I wanted to confront him on the spot, but I was conscious of and considerate of the child seated in the cart. In the end, I reasoned that there was no adequate way to deal with this unfortunate experience. But that didn't change the effect it had on me. My heart was pounding.

Next, my emotions raced from sadness to anger when I realized that the man was unmoved by what his child had just said. He gave me a haughty look, as if to say, "I taught my son well." Was it my

How could a child so young know such a dirty, despicable word? How? Why? What kind of "jerk" would teach such words to a baby?

imagination, or had he actually looked toward his son with a sense of pride that the child had learned how to use that nasty word so well? How could he not apologize for such an affront? How could he move on as if nothing had happened? Stunned, angry, and hurt, I had no recourse but to return to the task of shopping for my grandmother.

I was only fourteen when this incident occurred, but I was mature enough to realize how very wrong it was. As I struggled to understand how such a thing could happen, I came to the conclusion that racism is a learned behavior. Here was a man who had obviously taught his son how to say that word and, in the process, had made the child believe that Blacks were inferior creatures—just niggers. The mere thought of someone teaching their children to hate and to learn one of the most offensive and inflammatory racial slurs in the English language boggled my mind.

But I couldn't just stand there in the middle of the aisle, paralyzed with hurt and absorbing the shock of the moment. Forcing back the tears, I pulled myself together and continued the task before me. The tears had not been for me, but for the child. I knew that he was destined to grow up in ignorance and go on to teach others to hate on the basis of his own learned prejudice and racism.

In that one fleeting moment, my previously color-blind world was shattered, and I knew that we had a long way to go before embracing the dream of Dr. Martin Luther King, Jr., who had urged all men to judge each other, not by the color of their skin, but by the content of their character.

Afterward, similar incidents were to occur in the Jonathan Street area of my beloved hometown of Hagerstown. Most of the Blacks of the town lived in that area, Jonathan Street being a main artery that cut through the heart of the city and the Black community.

I had been born in Hagerstown, but my mother and I had moved away to Washington, D.C., during my elementary- and middle-school years. But it was the turbulent 1960's, and the nation's Capitol had become the center of a long and protracted struggle for Civil Rights. I recall the city erupting into civil unrest and violence following the assassination of Dr. Martin Luther King, Jr., on April 4, 1968. My mother returned home that day from her job at the post office near Union Station, and she proceeded to pack our suitcases and explain to me that we would be going to Grandmom's house for the weekend (or even longer, depending on when the rioting would end). As we were leaving town that day, we witnessed the mayhem erupting all around us. We saw anger in its rawest form: Teens and adults were hurtling bricks, bottles, and anything else they could get their hands on and smashing the storefront windows of local businesses. I remember seeing smoke billowing from the Congress Heights shopping area, as Mom continued to drive as fast as practical through the crowds, finally getting onto 295 Highway and leaving southeast Washington with a sigh of relief.

Upon reaching my grandmother's house a little more than an hour later, we glued our eyes to the television screen, watching the evening news reports about Washington, Detroit, Newark, and other cities that were erupting in flames. A shudder of fear swept over me as I began to wonder what would happen next. I wondered aloud if we might even see a race war begin. After all, with Dr. King gone, who would be the voice of moral clarity in a world gone mad? My mother and grandmother assured me that God would work it all out. I remember thinking that God had better hurry up, because the death of Dr. King was too much to take. Little did I realize that soon after Dr. King's assassination, America would lose yet another champion of Civil Rights, a man who seemed destined to become president—Senator Robert F. Kennedy.

When I watched the horrible scenes of Robert Kennedy's death, I remembered a happier time. I recalled the moment he had come to my neighborhood on the campaign trail. There he was, right across the street from my home, walking on the playground of Congress Heights Elementary School. I remembered making my way through the massive throngs of fans just to shake his hand. When I accomplished that, I felt like I had just touched royalty. It was a precious memory, a golden moment, but his life had now been snuffed out by an assassin's bullet. I was only thirteen at the time, but I had already witnessed so much destruction and carnage in my young life.

On November 22, 1963, I was sitting in my third-grade class at North Street School in Hagerstown. I remember my teacher, Mrs. Gilmore, going to the door to speak with someone. When she came back, she abruptly ended the class and turned on the television, asking us all to put our heads on our desks and pray for the President. Then, we watched together in silence as Walter Cronkite delivered the news that shook our nation and saddened the whole world: President John Fitzgerald Kennedy had been pronounced dead. I wept, Mrs. Gilmore wept, and my fellow students wept.

It took a moment for Mrs. Gilmore to compose herself, but then she consoled us, counseled us about the tragic event we had just witnessed, and prepared us to go home to be with our families. Somehow I sensed that day that our world would never be the same again.

This flashback to a nation in turmoil reflected how my own life had been stricken with the same kind of conflict. My mother, always diligent in her efforts to keep me on the straight and narrow path, became concerned about me toward the beginning of my adolescence. Sensing that I was getting caught up with the wrong crowd and developing wrong attitudes, she moved us back to that smaller-town atmosphere in Hagerstown.

Back then, Hagerstown was not considered to be the extra suburb of Washington and Baltimore that it is today. A small, bucolic town nestled in the Cumberland Valley and surrounded by the beautiful Blue Ridge Mountains, it is only a short distance from the Mason-Dixon line, which divides the North from the South. About ten miles to the south of town is the Antietam National Battlefield, the site of the bloodiest battle of the Civil War. Not far from there, over in neighboring Harper's Ferry, West Virginia, the fiery preacher and staunch abolitionist John Brown had been captured and hanged. I grew up in a place of history.

By the time I returned to live in Hagerstown, I was already learning by painful experience how the seeds of discord and bitterness birthed the ugliness of racism. Living in Hagerstown gave me a different perspective on how I could play a role in bringing people together from opposite sides racially and culturally. The very nature of my lifestyle contributed greatly to my inclination toward the ministry of reconciliation. I was living in an all-Black community where most of my family and friends resided, but I was attending an all-White private high school.

For the first two years, I was the only Black student at St. Maria Goretti High School. It was a small school, but big on love. Goretti, as

My mother, always diligent in her efforts to keep me on the straight and narrow path, became concerned about me toward the beginning of my adolescence.

we affectionately called the school, was made up of students who reached out to support each other. We were unique in that we were unafraid to band together through triumph and tragedy. Perhaps it was in our spiritual DNA to be so peculiar.

To understand in more detail, you have to consider the tragic, yet triumphant, real-life story of the school's namesake, Maria Goretti. Church history explains that Goretti was born Maria Teresa Goretti, on October 16, 1890, in Corinaldo, Italy. She was the third of six children, and her family became very poor after losing their farm. Maria's father died when she was nine, forcing the entire family to work for other farmers in the surrounding fields. Maria helped by doing the cooking, sewing, and cleaning. In their poverty, the family remained very close and constantly expressed a deep faith in God.

By age thirteen, Maria and her family moved to a small town known as LeFerriere. There they shared living quarters with another impoverished family, the Serenellis. Twenty-year-old Alessandro Serenelli took a deep and misguided sexual interest in young Maria. On July 5, 1902, while Maria was alone at home sewing, Alessandro began to sexually assault her. Desperately attempting to fight him off, she continually screamed, "No! It's a sin! God does not want it!" But he, driven by his passions, ignored her cries for him to stop. Now consumed with rage, he began choking young Maria, even as she continued to fight him off. Next, in his frustration, Alessandro took a knife and began stabbing Maria, plunging the knife into her body fourteen times before fleeing.

Maria's little sister found her bleeding and dying and called for help. Maria's mother and Alessandro's father carried Maria to the hospital, but her wounds were too severe to heal. Before dying, Maria said she forgave Alessandro and explained that she forgave him because she wanted to live in heaven.

The power of Maria's forgiveness lasted well beyond her short life. After serving thirty years in prison for killing Maria, Alessandro was released. He soon visited Maria's mother to beg her forgiveness. Maria's mother reasoned that if her daughter could forgive him on her deathbed, then she could also do it. Church records state that Alessandro and Maria Goretti's mother attended Mass together the next day and received Holy Communion. The story is told that Alessandro became a man of prayer, often referring to Maria Goretti as his "little saint."

Forgiveness and reconciliation, two essential elements in healing the broken spirit of humanity, were at work in the life of Maria Goretti, and that same spirit of love was evident in the small school that bears her name. The teachings beyond our academic curriculum stirred something within me that caused me to reach out and touch people from all racial, ethnic, and socioeconomic backgrounds. I was left with an abiding desire to see people come together. Also, the nuns and teachers reinforced my mother's values of faith, hope, and love.

> *Some of our most bitter enemies say they can hear the approaching hoofbeats of the four horsemen of the Apocalypse rushing into the heart of America.*

This positive learning environment enabled me to be free from the specter of racism. That, plus my college experiences at Oral Roberts University in Tulsa, Oklahoma, would further prepare me for understanding what was needed to bring healing between the races.

We got through the crisis generated by Dr. King's death and the deaths of John and Robert Kennedy. But our job was not finished by any means. We've come a long way, but amid the current chaos, some of our harshest critics and most bitter enemies say they can hear the approaching hoofbeats of the four horsemen of the Apocalypse rushing into the heart of America to bring about her demise. These enemies stand on the sidelines waiting for America to lose her soul, waiting to hear her heart beat no more. Then, they plan to sweep in like a flood and plunder the land, taking the spoils of America's grandeur.

But I believe and pray that God

is not through with these United States. I believe that while we are in the depths of our affliction, there is a seed of fruitfulness that is breaking through the tough soil, being watered by God's precious rain of blessings through the tears we shed for the hardships we bear. If we can grow through the weeds (the cares of this world) and the thorns (the deceptive seductions of this world) that seek to choke us, we will find ourselves developing, taking root in fertile soil, to blossom into our destiny, to be a people serving God.

Our afflictions are born out of resistance to very sound, wise, and heavenly instruction. We have failed to understand that God is leading us to a place of humility, lest we should become proud and haughty, forgetting that He is the source of our blessings. This was the precaution of the Jewish people, as they left Egypt, after spending four-hundred years in bondage there:

> *Make sure you don't forget GOD, your God, by not keeping his commandments, his rules and regulations that I command you today. Make sure that when you eat and are satisfied, build pleasant houses and settle in, see your herds and flocks flourish and more and more money come in, watch your standard of living going up and up—make sure you don't become so full of yourself and your things that you forget GOD, your God,*

the God who delivered you from Egyptian slavery;

the God who led you through that huge and fearsome wilderness, those desolate, arid badlands crawling with fiery snakes and scorpions;

the God who gave you water gushing from hard rock;

the God who gave you manna to eat in the wilderness, something your ancestors had never heard of, in order to give you a taste of the hard life, to test you so that you would be prepared to live well in the days ahead of you.

If you start thinking to yourselves, "I did all this. And all by myself. I'm rich. It's all mine!"—well, think again. Remember that GOD, your God, gave you the strength to produce all this wealth so as to confirm the covenant that he promised to your ancestors—as it is today.

If you forget, forget GOD, your God, and start taking up with other gods, serving and worshiping them, I'm on record right now as giving you firm warning: that will be the end of you; I mean it—destruction. You'll go to your doom—the same as the nations GOD is destroying before you; doom because you wouldn't obey the Voice of GOD, your God.   Deuteronomy 8:11-20, MSG

For further evidence, look to the transatlantic slave trade

of Blacks who were snatched from their native Africa and taken to foreign lands to serve four hundred years as someone's property, doing the bidding of their slavemasters. The African Diaspora extended to many countries: Brazil, Cuba, the Dominican Republic, England, Haiti, Holland, Portugal, Spain, the United States, and others. Yet, out of those four centuries of hardship, these people endured, finding their hope for freedom through a deep and abiding faith in God.

At the root of America's current racial tensions is the specter of this brutal and dehumanizing slave trade. The vestiges of slavery, the Jim Crow era, segregation, and the Civil Rights struggle still exert their divisive influence on our nation. While we can take pride in electing a Black man to the highest office in the land, we must continue to work toward racial reconciliation. There is still a subtle divide that stands in the way of our efforts to be one nation under God, indivisible, with liberty and justice for all.

In 1999, I embarked on an exciting assignment to the West African nation of Benin. My purpose was to report on the occasion of two African presidents apologizing for the role their ancestors played in perpetuating the slave trade. This historic event attracted descendants of slave traders, slave merchants, and slaves throughout the transatlantic slave-trading nations. It is important to understand that the goal of Benin's President Mathieu Kerekou was to provide an opportunity to spark reconciliation between Africans and African-Americans and between African-

Americans and Whites and use the model of forgiveness and reconciliation that resulted to quell tribal disputes and do away with political division, and to help all nations find healing from their past in order to be productive in the present and secure a brighter future.

Benin's Reconciliation and Development Conference may not have garnered international recognition, but it will never be forgotten for the visionary leadership of a man who sought to cross all political and religious divides, to create a dialogue on race that went beyond the surface. It was important enough that I want to devote the rest of this chapter to some reflections and personal observations from some of the men and women who participated in that significant moment in history. Allow me to direct your attention to this subject for the next few pages, to enlighten you about the apology that shook the hearts of men and women, charging them to keep sowing seeds of unity and keep weeding out the discord of racism.

During the historic Benin Racial Reconciliation Conference in December 1999, when the nation made a formal and public apology for its role in the transatlantic slave trade, Bishop David Perrin was asked to provide the African-American keynote address, when former U.S. Ambassador to the United Nations Andrew Young had to cancel, due to surgery. Perrin's speech was inspiring and transparent, as he shared the views of many African-Americans in regard to slavery and racism. In a subsequent interview, he discussed those views with me in more detail:

A Time for Healing

African Diaspora means the scattering of African people throughout the nations, most notably the forceful scattering. The Diaspora also includes Jewish people who have been forcibly scattered. Why is an apology necessary? We came here for matters and issues of the heart and soul. And I think that apologies grow out of the soul, out of the heart. So for me to say to you, "Oh, don't apologize," is wrong because it is your soul, your heart, your spirit that's leading you to know that something is wrong that needs to be made right. In this instance, President Mathieu Kerekou of the Republic of Benin felt moved in his heart to say, "This is something I need to do. It's something that my nation [needs to do], given that we had twelve million African people to leave these shores and to be scattered through-

> *It is your soul, your heart, your spirit that's leading you to know that something is wrong that needs to be made right.*

out the earth. And many of them died before they ever were there. I wasn't there originally, but it was my ancestors; it was those who sat in the position that I sit in now—kings, presidents, leaders."

Is an apology for slavery a sham? Well, I think, if you have a political agenda, if you already your-self have a predetermined agenda, then the sham is that you want more than an apology; you want more out of the apology than the apology is. Then indeed it's a sham. But if I sincerely, genu-inely say to you, "I'm sorry," then from there whatever is possible becomes possible because of the renewed integrity that exists between us.

How does it heal in America? In the back of the minds of African-Americans and perhaps Blacks throughout the Diaspora is the haunting possibility that indeed this dastardly deed was done by our own people. We are quick to accuse White people, and we have always said, "White people, you're mean, you're evil, you're wicked, you're prejudiced, you're bigoted," but, not wanting to accuse Africans, not wanting to say, "You played some part," I think that we pushed it all the way back into our subconscious mind, never wanting to deal with it, never wanting to face the reality that it was a triangle, that it took three. There were buyers, there were sellers, and there were those that were persecuted.

A Time for Healing

And what President Kerekou has done for all of us has produced a level of inner healing, to accept that my African brothers and sisters did sell us into slavery. They were very much responsible. We've gotten to a place in America where we can live with or without the apology. We didn't come here in tears, crying for an apology. We have dealt with our inner pain, but the fact that an apology has been given, is just like icing on the cake. It's like lifting a burden or veil because we're not waiting for an apology, but the fact that someone, out of their own integrity, is willing to offer it is just so refreshing. It's just like cool, refreshing water.

I'm a pastor, and I believe God is up to something. God will always do something in a small way, in some obscure place like Bethlehem or Nazareth (*"Can any good thing come out of Nazareth?"* [John 1:46]). Why in Benin, of all places? There was no media coverage of the event, and yet God did something momentous. I believe that this is His signature. I think that the Republic of Benin, not the summit in Ghana, not in Nigeria, not some of the great sub-Saharan countries, a president that's described as being one of the most lone men in Africa but with a conviction that God is moving. I think God's up to something, something awfully good!

> *When I allow myself to be vulnerable, then I am able to get over the intellectual and political approach and get to a deeper level.*

President Kerekou is a man of purpose, a man of destiny, and he's not going to be satisfied until he achieves all that God wants. His wife apologized to the members of the Congressional Black Caucus in America. They didn't respond favorably and support the reconciliation process. They have failed to embrace President Kerekou's efforts to be reconciled and seek development of his country. He believes that his country and other African nations are under a curse for their part, their role, in slavery. America has not apologized to Blacks for slavery, nor has it apologized to Native American Indians, and I think Kerekou is saying: "Well, why should America lead the way in terms of integrity?" And so he's taking the lead.

God has made me extremely transparent. I deal with issues

A Time for Healing

of the heart, not heady scholastic or political matters. When I allow myself to be vulnerable, then I am able to get over the intellectual and political approach and get to a deeper level.

I have three principles of reconciliation. The first is with my spouse. Every single week, you ask if you did something to hurt or offend. "Have I done something knowingly or unknowingly?" What it keeps you from doing is developing roots of bitterness, and so you clean that away.

The first principle is to know that reconciliation is something you have to do daily. Don't let the sun go down on your anger or on your wrath. And most of us, the reason we're stuck, the relationship between Pakistan and India, between Ireland and England, the anger that takes place in America with kids shooting kids in schools, we must learn the art again of checking with each other, and being willing to say, day by day, "I'm sorry if I offended you."

The second principle of reconciliation involves sibling rivalry, breakdown between brothers and also parents. We've been separated from our people for three hundred and fifty years. And to think that we could just walk into Africa and say, "It's going to be all right." Some people may never accept the apology. The apology that is extended here today is no small thing. The forgiveness that is extended here today is no small thing.

I have a confession to make. They thought that we would not allow ourselves to think for centuries. They thought that actually our African brothers and sisters deliberately, by an act of their will, for the purposes of greed and self-advantage, would dare to sell their brothers and sisters into slavery and never feel that we could feel the pain and anguish of our ancestors here. But we've seen the places where our brothers and sisters were being captured, separated from their families, murdered, and whipped. And we felt the open sores to our back. I thought about one of the most vivid conversations I ever had with my grandmother.

My grandmother wasn't born into slavery. She said, "David, I'll tell you a story about slavery." She said, "White folks used to take the girls and put them in a shed with their dogs so that the dogs could mate with them." She said, "It's not possible for dogs to mate with people, and so it was just sport. It was fun for them, because they considered us to be animals, and animals should mate with animals."

I looked in the faces of my brothers and sisters, and seated right in this room are those who could not eat at lunch counters, those who were beaten and whipped during the Civil Rights Movement. In my wife's hometown of Danville, Virginia, her folks were part of the movement. They were beaten by police with billy clubs. They whipped the women until their breasts burst. Men were attacked by dogs, and we ask ourselves, "Could Africans have known? Could Africans have sold us into this kind of life and then have turned their backs on us?" Some say it's not true, and I have said in my heart, "It is not true." I have sat by those who lived through Hitler's terror, and they said, "It never happened!" And, President Kerekou, the reason we love you is that you have said what no one else has been willing to say, that we, as Africans, have had a role, have had a part. Without a seller, there could be no buyers. You have stood when no one has asked you, when no one has requested you to come forward and to take responsibility. This, Mr. President, is noble! What we do today is only through what God has shown us. It is only through what He has modeled for us that we have been able to forgive nasty White people, mean White people, racist White people, preju-diced White people, bigoted White people, and now it is by His grace and it is by His power that we are able to reach out to our African brothers

and to our African sisters and to say to you that
because of the love of God and the faith that we
have in Christ, we forgive it all. We forgive it all.
We forgive it all.

Alastair Geddes, a pastor, businessman, and founder
of Impact International, a Christian organization that
provides relief for the poor living in Africa, was also a par-
ticipant in the event. Alastair, a man who takes pride in
being born in Scotland, the birthplace of golf, has a deep
respect and appreciation for Africa, and he lived there for
nearly twenty years before moving to the United States to
become the vice-president of Christ For The Nations. In
his endearing Scottish accent, Alastair shared his wonderful
story with me:

> I don't know that I felt guilty until I got here. I
> mean, I wanted to be a part of the process of rec-
> onciliation. I knew there was a problem. I knew
> that Black people and White people had a prob-
> lem with each other. I knew there was a need for
> reconciliation, but I did not realize the depth of
> what the slave trade … what it was all about.
> I don't think people of any race fully know the
> depth of this thing we call the slave trade, this
> atrocity, and the deep hurt and the guilt that
> it caused. And from the side of the African-
> Americans and the Diaspora—in Brazil and the

A Time for Healing

Caribbean—but also from the side of guilt from the White people, all I can tell you is that as we've been discussing this whole thing of slavery, when we stood on the beach in Benin and at the Gate of No Return, and I heard the water lapping, and I saw African-Americans get their pant legs wet and their shoes covered in water because they were just standing there looking out to sea, looking towards America, I began to weep.

Now, usually, when a man of fifty-three years of age cries, it means something is going on in the inside, and I really can't tell you what it is. I didn't do anything to African-Americans, but I think that in the whole process I realize that my ancestors profited from this, like people all over the world. And I think seeing people that I've grown to love, Black people, African-Americans, I began to realize the hurt

> *I didn't do anything to African-Americans, but ... I realize that my ancestors profited from this, like people all over the world.*

that they're going through. In fact, I'm even hurting, and it hurts deeply. I don't know that every African-American will understand what this thing called reconciliation is. It seems like a very long process.

I've been working on this road of reconciliation since my wild days as a young man in Rhodesia during the 1960's and early 70's. Healing is a long process. The average person is probably not even aware of their own hurt. This hurt comes out through aggression, through hate, through bitterness. I think many African-Americans have a chip on their shoulder, and the reason for it is that they're not reconciled. No healing has taken place.

What I've learned here is that Blacks have always blamed Whites. And certainly Whites did wrong. They were slave traders, and it was evil. It was an abomination. But what has been learned here is that although Whites bought slaves, the condition of Africa was that the people of Benin, Ghana, Senegal, and Togo sold their brothers. There are some eighty million Black people in Brazil, and Black people in Brazil are just as hurt as African-Americans. So it's a big picture.

Only six or seven percent of all Africans sold into slavery went to the United States. We who are living in America sort of take it for granted that is was one hundred percent, b. But the vast majority of slaves went to other places.

Now we talk about the guilt. Sure, many of us feel guilty. But you don't really sense the guilt until you've made a visit here. What's helped us all get through the slavery, get through the guilt, get through the pain, get through the hurts, get through the discrimination, get through the race issues in America is faith. What's interesting is that when slaves first left these shores, there was no faith, no healing through God, no relevance to Jesus Christ. But what they had was a form of voodoo, or animism, and they had no faith in God. But now the President of Benin is a man of faith and undoubtedly a man of Christ. That's been part of the healing process.

What about people without faith? Why should they care? In a sense, it's very difficult. But I do believe that everyone is hurting. You don't need to be a person of faith to hurt. You do need to be a person of faith to get healing from your hurt. And I think faith helps you to understand where guilt comes from. A lot of people in America today don't see guilt for what it is. They put it off as something else. We need to take ownership of our problems. I think both White people have shoved it aside and also the African-Americans, who say, "Well, the White man did it to me. Therefore, I have a right to be bitter." But you know what? Bitterness kills. Bitterness eats up the soul. It causes broken relationships. Really, it is time for healing.

I guess, when I was a policeman in Rhodesia, something deep down inside of me was saying that the racial attitude there was not right. I was raised in Scotland, and we didn't have any Black people there. The only Blacks who came there were university students. So my background was not racist. But then I went to Rhodesia in the 1960's.

I was very young, an only child, and I wanted to see the world. I had always had a need to be accepted, and I guess when you get six thousand miles from home, and you're in a foreign country, in the middle of Africa, what do you do with your life? There's

> *"I have a right to be bitter." But ... bitterness kills. Bitterness eats up the soul. It causes broken relationships. ... It is time for healing.*

no Mommy there to help you. You want to fit in, so when I arrived there, I was taught how to deal with Black people: "Don't give them too much." "Don't do this." "Don't do that." And in the end, that kind of prejudice takes over. I became a racist, and I did many things that I regret to Black people who were under me. It was a very difficult situation.

A traumatic thing took place in my life, when I was caught in a firefight, and bullets were whizzing by me. It made me realize that I needed a relationship with Jesus Christ, and it changed my life and my perceptions of all men.

It was faith that brought me to the realization that what I was doing was wrong. Here I was, a security officer with Ian Smith, the White Rhodesian prime minister. Only faith could have brought this kind of turnaround in my life. Let me tell you: God changed me from a racist to a relationship person, and that was a complete turnaround.

This reconciliation gives me hope. If we can take this message of hope to every American community, we can cross the divide. It's time to get rid of the guilt (if you're White), and it's time to get rid of the anger (if you're Black). Come together and see that there is hope, and let reconciliation begin."

David Hall of Minneapolis, Minnesota, is a White American who works with university students in Kenya, Ghana, and Uganda. He also does small-business development in Africa in the hope of creating a dynamic middle class, educated in the universities of Africa, that can become the economic generator for Africa. His work is called Africa Partners. He shared his thoughts on reconciliation with me:

> I lived in Africa for eighteen years, but I didn't know what the African-Americans were feeling about Africans. I also didn't realize how much of a role the Africans had in selling their ancestors into slavery. So I wanted to know more about that, and I've learned that they did have a very significant role. The President of Benin realizes this and wants to help reconcile our past.
>
> The African-Americans feel like they don't have roots, they don't have a name, and they don't have a place that they can go to. In the Old Testament, God gave Israel a chunk of land. So I think there is a theology of place, so they can know God in the context of history. And I think that it's important for African-Americans to be able to come back here to Africa and visit the land they came from.
>
> Why should White Americans care about slav-

ery? Well, just being in Ghana for thirteen years and going down to the two slave forts, Elmina and Cape Coast Fort, the staging areas for the slaves waiting for the ships to come in, helped me to realize that our hands are dirty. It was the economic incentives that caused the Whites to be involved "big time" in the slave trade. Being here at this conference, I think one of the things that was left out was just how much the Whites were involved in the slave trade. They were the big players because they had the economic power to provide the incentives to bring the slaves to America.

I think the message to White America is reconciliation. For their part in the problem, they need to repent. The Africans need to repent for their part, and the Europeans need to repent for their part. Everyone needs a clean slate.

The impact of slavery continues. All of the other continents in the world have progressed against poverty—all except Africa. The Africans don't have the same economic opportunities as the rest of the world. One reason is that they're looked upon as inferior because they're Black, and Whites need to come to Africa to find out for themselves that it's just not true. They need to learn how to invest in Africa economically, as part of the reconciliation. Otherwise it's not a true reconciliation.

At the same time, we must realize that Africans can teach us something about their worldview. Whites are much more pagan in their worldview than Africans. Our focus is on self and individualism. We know who we are by what we own and what we know. The Africans know who they are because of who they belong to, and that's much more biblical. They know who they are because of their connection with their families and hometowns. You don't ask an African what he does when you are introduced to him. You ask him where he's from. With Whites, you ask, "What do you do?" because that's where their identity is. And so we need Africans to minister to us. I bring doctors and professionals to help Africans in their small-business development, but it's the Africans who really minister to the Anglos.

I believe that an apology and forgiveness create a win-win situation because we need each other. We need the African-Americans desperately, and we need the Africans desperately, because they have a spirituality that Whites don't have. Who gives thanks to God at the Grammys for their successes? Who gives Him thanks for a touchdown on the football field? It's not the Whites; it's the African-Americans, and it's because they have a spirituality that we Whites don't have. They are, however, in between world-views. There is an African component to their worldview, but they are also pressed by the Anglo worldview to become a selfish, individualistic person that they don't really want to be, because it's not biblical. The biblical context is that we are community people.

COMINAD, or the Cooperative Missions Network of the African Dispersion, is the brainchild of Brian Johnson. He formed the organization to mobilize African-American churches to get involved in missionary work throughout the Black Diaspora. Johnson and his co-director, Jack Gaines, work with hundreds of volunteers from all races to develop programs of reconciliation and forgiveness. In a discussion about racial reconciliation, Jack Gaines explained to me:

> *The Africans know who they are because of who they belong to, and that's much more biblical.*

All the facts of history haven't been revealed, and when we don't understand all of the facts of history, we attempt to implement strategies to deal with the issues that have come out of history. Our strategies, therefore, are ineffective. So coming here and gaining an understanding of what Africa contributed to slavery and what Europe contributed gives us a balanced perspective. Now we can begin to deal with the issues out of that era.

I've always gotten along with people. As a young boy, some of my best friends were White, and when my father started a Little League baseball team, it was kind of reverse racism. We had two White boys playing with us, and when we were going to a Black neighborhood to play, the two White boys couldn't go. My father took a stand (at a point in my life that helped me deal with the race issue) by saying that if the White boys couldn't play, then the team couldn't play.

Jack Gaines went on to play professional baseball with the Pittsburgh Pirates and the Boston Red Sox. He experienced the scourge of racism during his nine years as a major league pitcher and dealt with terrible acts of segregation. While traveling with the team, he was often told by restaurant owners that he couldn't sit down to eat with the team in the main dining area but would have to be served in the kitchen. Through those very painful years, he still believed that reconciliation between the races was an ideal that could someday be achieved. He said, "I feel it's an opportunity to do something significant that will benefit the world. The opportunity to establish a reconciliation that works is very significant."

Brian Johnson is a native of Detroit, Michigan. He now resides in Virginia Beach, Virginia, where he operates COMINAD. Brian launched this unique missionary group to get more African-American people involved in missions work. In fact, the mission of COMINAD is to mobilize Christians with African roots to reach the world, especially the unreached, with the gospel of Jesus Christ. Brian said:

> I've been working on reconciliation in Africa for several years now, so reconciliation is just what I'm about. Apology for slavery? I think that we're obligated when someone asks for forgiveness to extend forgiveness. In our situation as African-Americans in our generation, we've been blessed a great deal. The tragedy of the slave trade still lingers on here, as it does in America. There are tribes who were sold into slavery who still hold animosity against the other tribe which sold them. That hatred has been going on for three or four hundred years. Now if we don't do something about it, it's going to erupt in all-out

> *Our children are simply pointing fingers at the White man. "The White man's responsible," and that gives them an excuse not to perform to their ability.*

tribal warfare. Allow any type of problem to happen, any instability, and suddenly revenge will be sought on those who hurt each other so many years ago.

Back in the 1960's we learned how to quickly disarm the White man by making him feel that he was responsible for the enslavement of Blacks and all of the problems that happened to the Black race since that point. Now that has become a great problem for us Black Americans, because the only way we can get freedom from our problems is to take ownership of our own sins. If we can blame someone else for our problems and never take ownership for them, we will never be victorious in life or live a responsible life.

What is happening in our communities today? Our children are simply pointing fingers at the White man.

"The White man's responsible,'" and that gives them an excuse not to perform to their ability. We have to take ownership. If we don't take ownership, forgiveness will not happen. Our lives will not get better, because of our own problems.

This opportunity that we have here shakes us up, because it lets us know that Blacks were involved in the slave trade as well as Whites. That creates some problems with us, because we kind of had the White man where we wanted him, and now we have to deal with another aspect of this. People just like us sold our people into slavery. And how do we reconcile this? Do we say to the Africans, "We forgive you?" If so, then we have to forgive the White man too. We have to do things equally. So I think, in the long run, because of this balancing act, which I think the Lord has created, we have to realize that we must have the heart to forgive.

In their desire to expand the ministry of reconciliation, Johnson and Gaines, along with Benin's President Mathieu Kerekou, initiated a program called Adopt-A-Village. The initiative urges African-American churches to literally adopt villages throughout Benin. The church members help the villages by sending donations to build schools, wells, local credit unions, homes, and more. Through the

Adopt-A-Village program, African-Americans are able to visit the villages and develop lasting friendships with the villagers. The program is a phenomenal way for African-Americans and Africans to demonstrate the ministry of reconciliation. It shows how the love of Jesus Christ helps us overcome problems caused by race and the pain of the past.

Johnson and Gaines point out in the book *African-American Experience in World Mission: A Call Beyond Community:*

> The same principles that have worked between Africans and African-Americans can work in Bosnia and Serbia. They can work for Rwanda and Burundi. They can work in Northern Ireland. They can work anywhere in the world where there is conflict.

Johnson notes that the one thing the world truly needs is reconciliation between peoples, but he adds that the key is forgiveness, explaining:

> In the Bible, when Adam and Eve sinned against God, it was God who initiated forgiveness. And it was God who sent Jesus Christ to take man's sin away and clear the way for reconciliation with Him. Jesus, who was completely innocent, said of those who crucified Him, "Father, forgive

them, for they know not what they do." Forgiveness is the key, and only victims really have control over granting forgiveness.

President Mathieu Kerekou, Brian Johnson, Jack Gaines and hundreds of other courageous and loving believers have made great contributions to winning the war on racism. They continue to introduce the world to the unfailing leadership of Jesus Christ. However, there are still extremely malevolent forces at work in the world. Despite the significant impact of Benin's reconciliation effort, slavery and oppression are great evils that continue to plague the world. Many people refuse to accept the reality that a modern-day slave trade is being conducted ruthlessly throughout the world, without, for the most part, adequate repudiation from the international community. One need only look to the barbaric slave trade in Sudan.

Cal R. Bombay of Toronto, Canada, is vice-president of Missions for Crossroads Christian Communications. Having served as a missionary in Kenya and Uganda for seventeen years, he is very familiar with the current slave trade being conducted in that war-ravaged country. In his book *Let My People Go* (Sisters, Oregon: Multnomah Publishers, 1998), Bombay documents his true story of present-day persecution and slavery. He recounts how in 1997 he participated in a mission to buy the freedom of hundreds of Christian slaves in Sudan. He explains how Islamic fundamentalists in the north capture women and children (many of them Christian) and sell them to other northern Muslims as servants and concubines:

> There they live on table scraps and are forced to convert to Islam. Their stories are devastating, yet their capacity for hope is an inspiration to the world.
>
> — Cal Bombay in *Let My People Go*

Bombay urges readers to take action to bring an end to the despicable slave trading of the twenty-first century, writing:

> Pray for the beleaguered people of the various tribes of southern Sudan. Ask the Lord what you should do about it. Imagine yourself in the situation. Make it personal by realizing how you would feel if it was your husband, wife, or children who were being beaten, raped, treated like animals, and, all too often, killed. Contact your local news media and ask why so little is being said about such atrocities. Ask that they do their own research and disseminate their findings. Give them a copy of the United Nations report by Dr. Biro. Financially support any mission or agency which is trying to feed the starving and/or free slaves, or which is working to expose these evils to the eyes of the world community.
>
> — Cal Bombay in *Let My People Go*

Carnal man demands everything from everybody. We hurt people, offend people, and refuse to apologize for our misdeeds. The problems between all races and ethnic groups could be healed if we would follow the model of forgiveness that Jesus Christ has given us. It sounds like too simplistic a remedy for a very complex problem, but if we would attempt to do what Christ calls us to do, I firmly believe that we would see development along all the lines of reconciliation. We would see communities coming together, people of all different colors and nationalities working side by side.

The country of Singapore imposed a law that all racial and ethnic groups must live together—Muslims with Christians, Jews, and Gentiles all living side by side. And it seems to work. Could we not do the same?

It is time for some modern-day Josephs to return to Africa and offer a helping hand to those in great

> *The problems between all races and ethnic groups could be healed if we would follow the model of forgiveness that Jesus Christ has given us.*

need. Some African-Americans are already hard at work at reconciling with their brothers and sisters. Calvary Evangelical Baptist Church of Portsmouth, Virginia, is involved in helping a remarkable village in the jungles of Benin. They have gone beyond institutional adoption. They are truly developing one-on-one relationships with the people of Akpali-Xpevi Jesu Lome village.

The villagers say that the "Jesu Lome" part of the name was added after they asked Jesus to come into the village and establish Himself as their chief, and the name means that the village is in His hands. Romaine Zannou, the pastor of President Mathieu Kerekou, said the work in the village began five years ago. Zannou explained that the Lord was speaking to him and a small group of his friends about expanding His kingdom and going beyond the basic message of salvation.

Romaine recalls the first time he came into the village. It was all "bush country," he says. There were no roads, and it was one of the dirtiest places in Africa he had ever visited. The people were desperate, without hope, and felt that no one cared about them. They hardly wore clothes. Romaine, a total stranger to the villagers, says his group came with empty hands but a full heart of love and was ready to serve the people. He said, "I asked the villagers, 'Have you heard about big cities like Paris, New York, Oslo, or Washington, D.C.?' Then I asked them if they believed their cities could rise to that level. They said, 'No, no!' But I told them, 'I'm here to tell you that they can.' I told them that God could bring them hope, and they asked me how."

This wise pastor began to explain his mission by tapping into the people's imagination and desire. He said, "Let's start by building a big tower. What do you think we should start with? Let's build the roof first and then add the walls." They said, "But on what will the roof rest?" He answered, "You're right. We should build a foundation first. But it must be a firm foundation in order to build a great village. There are two foundations required. The first is to love God with all your heart, your might, and your strength. The second is to love each other. If we start with this foundation, we can build a great village."

Looking at the thick vegetation in the jungle where the villagers lived, Romaine added, "We have all this bush around us. Do you think we can go into the bush and start sowing corn now?" They said, "No, we have to clear the land first." "Again, you are right," he told them. "But clearing away the bush will require the use of tools." Then he added, "There are also weeds that can hinder our development, and they need to be cleared away: fear, hatred, jealousy, greed, and wickedness. Tools will be needed to remove these weeds. And the weeds that are in our hearts cannot be taken away with human tools. We need a tool that is called the Word of God. I don't care what religion you belong to, because we're not here to talk about your religion; we're here to talk to you about your development.

"There is a precious seed that can change your life, the

seed of the will of God. Will you all come together and meet with my friends from the city who will be telling you about the Word of God? They will tell you how to love Jesus. They will teach you the Word of God and teach you how to love like Jesus, live like Jesus, and be like Jesus, and they will also teach you how to love each other. We would love to see you be the people who live and think like Jesus. Would you be interested in that?" And they answered yes.

The core of their message was to love God and love your neighbor and get away from wickedness.

Romaine and his four friends came three times a week to love the people. Instead of just preaching the Word of God to them, they started reading from the Scriptures about Jesus. These five men of purpose allowed the villagers to see Jesus in them by being willing to serve and love the people. They showed them how to love. Then, Romaine explains, "Before long, the villagers began to ask, 'Why are you doing all this for us?' We told them, 'Jesus sent us here to love you because He loved us first. If you want to know Him, we can introduce you to Him.'

A Time for Healing

The villagers said they wanted to know Him. So the villagers began meeting with Jesus every morning, reading the Word of God. Everyone in the village came to know Jesus Christ in a personal and loving way."

These people transformed their village from a Hollywood jungle stereotype into a model area that now boasts not only of sufficient crops, but also of a bank, a road, and a school. The gospel is alive in Akpali, people to people. The area is clean now. The chief of the village says that the story of brotherly love must be told. He says that the five friends from Cotonou came out to teach them how to love God. He says, "Their message transformed and changed our lives. The core of their message was to love God and love your neighbor and get away from wickedness. And I can tell you before the arrival of the five men, this was a divided place. Husbands were beating their wives, and there was hatred here. Jesus came here with a divine broom and swept away all the wicked things that existed here. Now we get together and pray, and we work together.

"We have also taken it upon ourselves to go into the neighboring villages and share our message, and other villages are embracing the wonderful message. We have come to understand that we have this responsibility to share the message. That's how we're going to work out our problems here so other villages can be touched.

"We continue to work on building our village. Today we have clean water, because God's people helped us build a well. Another blessing is our local school for our kids.

Before we built a school here, our children had to walk five miles to school. Now they can walk a few yards to attend school, thanks to God's people. We are developing an agricultural business. All of this is possible because we are blessed by God and the work started by these five men and the people of the Calvary Evangelical Church in Portsmouth, Virginia."

Bishop David Perrin of Global Missions says that Akpali is a shining example of what the ministry of reconciliation can accomplish. He urges people in the United States to understand that it takes a whole village to raise one child. "Here's a place (Akpali) where people have come together to say, 'Let's be a people. Let's stand together and build our village.' In America, everyone has become their own little enclave, living their lives in isolation behind their closed doors. What we see here in Akpali is an extension of reconciliation. We can embrace a village and be embraced by that village. There is a mutual sharing now and a global need for all of us to work together."

God's Word tells us:

> *Reckless words pierce like a sword, but the tongue of the wise brings healing.* Proverbs 12:18, NIV

There are many Africans who put their African-American brothers and sisters to a biblical comparison. President Kerekou and other leaders suggest that the journey of African-Americans is very similar to the story of Joseph.

A Time for Healing

While in Benin, I was fortunate to be among a small group of African-Americans who had an audience with President Kerekou. During our meeting, I asked President Kerekou what message he had for the United States. He replied, "Please tell Americans that we still see America as a beacon of hope for the poor nations of the world."

As a follow-up, I asked, "Mr. President, what is your message to African-Americans?" His response was, "Tell the African-Americans to no longer think of themselves as victims, but as victors. We consider them to be the modern-day Josephs, who helped build the global economy we enjoy today."

What President Kerekou stated that day was beyond statesmanship; it was profound. I, along with those who listened intently, was stunned by his wisdom. In one statement, he had summed up the African-American experience with blazing precision. His words were liberating and ringing with the hope that all African-Americans would jettison their feelings of victimization and embrace the reality of being victors. Like Joseph, the African-American was sold into captivity by his own brother, but emerged as a leader in the free world, helping to build the United States of America into the great nation and world leader it is today.

Kerekou's assertions can be traced through America's early beginnings. Historians say that when English settlers tried to establish America's first settlement in Jamestown,

Virginia, they were soon dying from disease and hunger. The inhospitable swampland and brackish water of the James River was threatening to doom their plans to develop a viable colony for England in the New World.

Then, when Black slaves arrived in Jamestown, the tiny settlement began to make a dramatic turnaround. The Africans knew how to live off the land and helped the settlers develop a better way of surviving the harsh elements. More importantly, the African slaves saw a plant they were familiar with in Benin—tobacco. They taught the English settlers how to cultivate tobacco, and that golden leaf became America's cash crop and the economic fuel for building a nation. The African slave had introduced the settlers to a path toward an adventurous life of freedom, and yet the joys of freedom would remain unattainable for the Black man in America for the next four hundred years. In that same period, America would significantly enhance her stature in the world at the expense of weary men and women who were forced into lives of servitude, providing their "owners" with free labor.

Like Joseph in the pit and the prison, the slaves of America endured injustice but continued to help build a nation. Eventually, after emancipation, Jim Crowism, Civil Rights and other hurdles, African-Americans are finally being recognized for their significant contributions to developing the global economy we enjoy today. Dr. Ernestine Rheems of Oakland, California, says that Joseph's painful experiences in the PIT actually made him a Prophet In Training.

A Time for Healing

There is so much for African-Americans to learn from Joseph. While slavery was indeed an ugly blight on our history, it did not and cannot keep us locked down as victims, for we are not victims but victors through Jesus Christ.

Later, Joseph's brothers were remorseful for selling him into captivity, and they were also fearful of how he would treat them now that his father had died and been buried:

> So they sent word to Joseph, saying, "Your father left these instructions before he died: 'This is what you are to say to Joseph: I ask you to forgive your brothers the sins and the wrongs they committed in treating you so badly.' Now please forgive the sins of the servants of the God of your father." When their message came to him, Joseph wept. ... Joseph said to them, "Don't be afraid. Am I in the place of God? You intended to harm me, but God intended

The Africans knew how to live off the land and helped the settlers develop a better way of surviving the harsh elements.

193

> *it for good to accomplish what is now being done,*
> *the saving of many lives."*
>
> Genesis 50:16-20, NIV

We have an obligation to forgive! Jesus said:

> *"For if you forgive men when they sin against you,*
> *your heavenly Father will also forgive you."*
>
> Matthew 6:14, NIV

Every year the Great Commission Global Network sponsors a seminar on missions. The goal is to inform and enlist more African-American churches into the ranks of those who have a burden to share the gospel with others. The group recently encouraged me to launch the Noble Desire Foundation that can help churches throughout the world. It follows the model of forgiveness that has been given to us by our Lord and Savior, Jesus Christ. His ministry of reconciliation teaches us how to bridge the cultural, ethnic, and religious divides that exist in the world today. It presents us with the opportunity to someday develop better relationships with people from different racial backgrounds. He taught us what to do before we lay our gift down at His altar:

> *"First be reconciled to your brother, and then come*
> *and offer your gift."* Matthew 5:24

A Time for Healing

We are accustomed, here in America, to funding organizations that are headed by leadership that is predominantly White, which gives people the impression that Black organizations are not to be trusted or are inept and inferior, and their ability to reach the world is inadequate. While that may be true in some cases, I have seen the profound impact that African-Americans have made throughout Africa. Even beyond the scope of missionary work, African-Americans, like President Barack Obama, Oprah Winfrey, Muhammad Ali, Stevie Wonder, Dr. Ben Carson, and others, have had a tremendous impact on the lives of people around the world.

To follow up on the Reconciliation and Development Conference, where President Kerekou apologized for the misdeeds of slavery, the Benin government embarked on an ambitious cultural program to further the cause of reconciliation. In 2002, Benin established the first International Gospel and Roots Festival. The heads of state sponsored the program as a continuation of the 1999 leadership conference, and both continue to have a ripple effect, not only in Benin, but throughout the entire continent.

Angelique Kidjo is Benin's first lady of song. This internationally acclaimed recording artist is known for exciting performances. But in Benin, she is also known for her compassion for Africa. As the honorary queen of the Gospel and Roots Festival, Angelique appealed to the Diaspora from the heart:

Dear friends from America and from other parts of the world, I am honored to be a part of this festival. It's about time that we start to get together, because we share the same roots. We share the same values. Slavery is a part of our history. We can't forget that. It has happened. Now is not the time to keep on asking, "Who's at fault? Why did it happen?" From now on we have to build up a new Black Diaspora. We are brothers and sisters.

> *All Americans are descendants of men and women who left their homelands, ... and emigrated to this new land ... in search of freedom.*

Our music and culture followed the slaves wherever they went. It helped them survive, and it's because of the music we can have this festival today. Music is the only language we all speak equally wherever we come from .... It doesn't matter the color of our skin. And modern music exists today because of the influence and input of the slaves. We have to use our music as part of our healing. We have to

196

start talking. It's not going to be easy. This is just the beginning of a long process.

We have been experiencing a century of division. Now, if we want to fill up the gap, for us to get together to be a power that the world has to recognize, we have to work together, hand in hand, in music, business, and faith. Africa is in turmoil with HIV/AIDS. There are so many problems we have to deal with in Africa, but with your help we can overcome anything. We've survived slavery; we can survive anything if we put our heart into it.

All Americans are descendants of men and women who left their homelands, dimmed by intolerance and cruel governments, and emigrated to this new land called America in search of brighter days, in search of freedom. Therefore, let us never forget each group's struggle. Let us never forget the Native American, who resided on this rich tapestry of land before us. And we cannot afford to forget our relationship with God, who carried us through our weary years. It is a relationship that has been forged through a covenant sealed with blood, beginning with Abraham and concluding with Jesus Christ, who redeems all mankind:

"For God so loved the world that He gave His only

begotten son, that whoever believes in Him should not perish but have everlasting life."   John 3:16

This scripture is the cornerstone of our faith and the stumbling block for those who would rather reject it than accept the forgiveness, guidance, and everlasting love of an eternal God. Let us choose to stay true to our faith in God, as we hang on to the world as it spins wildly around. Let us never lose our firm grip on His Word, seeking to glorify Him in everything we do.

This, my friends, is *America's Hope*.

Chapter Eleven

Faith Triumphs in Trouble

Love is patient, love is kind. It does not envy, it does not boast, it is not proud. It is not rude, it is not self-seeking, it is not easily angered, it keeps no record of wrongs.   1 Corinthians 13:4-5, NIV

Hope is defined as "a belief in a positive outcome related to events and circumstances in one's life. Hope implies a certain amount of despair, wanting, wishing, suffering, or perseverance—i.e., believing that a better or positive outcome is possible even when there is some evidence to the contrary. To wish for something with the expectation of the wish being fulfilled" (Wikipedia, the online Encyclopedia).

Hope is filled with expectation. We should learn to live our lives filled with what Oral Roberts described in the now-famous phrase "Expect a miracle"—expecting something good to happen to us this very day, this very hour. Creflo Dollar says:

Expectation is the breeding ground of miracles. Stick your neck out in expectation that God will provide. Become like David and run toward the enemy; don't shrink in fear, but move forward with hope. Celebrate the goodness of God and expect a miracle, new ideas for fulfilling God's will.

Now faith is the substance of things hoped for, the evidence of things not seen.　　　Hebrews 11:1

So, what kind of hope do you have? What do you hope to accomplish? You've got to keep hope alive! Hope is confident and produces favorable consequences. You've got to hope for things that are good for you and see yourself accomplishing those goals, regardless of the circumstances surrounding you. Hope will help deliver what you've put your faith into accomplishing. Treat the ending as if it were the beginning. In other words, see yourself as you want to be, not as you are:

Therefore, having been justified by faith, we have peace with God through our Lord Jesus Christ, through whom also we have access by faith into this grace in which we stand, and rejoice [to feel joy or great delight] *in HOPE of the glory of God*

[worshipful praise, honor, and thanksgiving]. *And not only that, but we also glory in tribulations, knowing that tribulation produces perseverance; and perseverance, character; and character, hope* [an unbroken circle of blessings. The wheel of faith in constant motion, producing hope to hope, faith to faith, love to love, glory to glory, man to God through Jesus Christ. The proof that the wheel or circle of hope exists is in what Paul discusses here]. *Now hope does not disappoint, because the love of God has been poured out in our hearts by the Holy Spirit who was given to us.*
Romans 5:1-5

> *You've got to hope for things that are good for you and see yourself accomplishing those goals, regardless of the circumstances surrounding you. Hope will help deliver what you've put your faith into accomplishing.*

Let's break this down. Despite the fact that I always strive to remain optimistic about life through prayer, singing, and listening to praise music, I can still feel like all my hope is gone and that my positive attitude in life got up and went. Circumstances on my job, in my marriage, and in my relationships with my children can sometimes produce feelings of anxiety. When anxiety bubbles up on the inside of me, I feel that a sense of doom and gloom begins to rise up within me. Instead of allowing peace to be still or having the outlook that whatever comes my way, it is well with my soul, I find myself slipping into darkness, becoming distrustful or unfaithful, doubting myself and suspecting that God is no longer working things out for my good. Yes, I go through this from time to time. Beyond the smile on my face, there are times when I'm smiling on the outside but frowning or crying on the inside.

I am sharing all of this with you because I know you've been through it too, or possibly are going through it right now. In these tough times, who wouldn't go through some painful experiences? But here's the deal: God knows and hears our distress signal, which is why Paul could confidently say, "Now hope does not disappoint!"

Just like David, you can run toward your enemy and not retreat, knowing that the battle is the Lord's. Use the tools and talent God has bestowed upon you, then watch Goliath (your giant problems) fall down dead. The force of faith being applied in your life will compel people to see and believe:

A man shall eat well by the fruit of his mouth, but the soul of the unfaithful feeds on violence.

Proverbs 13:2

Set a guard, O LORD, over my mouth; keep watch over the door of my lips. Do not incline my heart to any evil thing. Psalm 141:3-4

Do we really matter on this earth? Yes, we do. We live in God, and God lives in us. Therefore, everything we do is important, and it matters. Every time we forgive, the universe changes; every time we reach out and touch a heart or a life, the world changes; with every kindness and service, seen or unseen, God's purposes are accomplished, and nothing will be the same again. Therefore, from this moment forward, live your life dependent upon God. Let Him have a relationship with you. Embrace Christ; engage the world. Go and make a difference.

I hope you develop a hunger for reconciliation and get involved in the Jesus Revolution. It is not a revolution that will overthrow anything, or, if it does, it will do so in ways we could never contrive in advance. Instead, it will be the quiet daily powers of dying and serving and loving and laughing, of simple tenderness and unseen kindness, because if anything matters, then everything matters.

The United States of America is undergoing an identity crisis. We are victims of identity theft. Like a thief in the night, America's enemies have quietly stolen into our country and tampered with our national DNA—that we are one nation under God, indivisible, with liberty and justice for all. Our country's motto is emblazoned on our American currency. Pull a dollar bill out of your wallet, and there it is: "In God we trust." Yet there have been and continue to be designs on the part of some to remove any reference to God. Allow me to remind you that the birth of America came about because a band of pilgrims were searching for a new land where they could form a new country founded on religious freedom. Unfortunately, in our modern twenty-first century era,

> *Like a thief in the night, America's enemies have quietly stolen into our country and tampered with our national DNA— that we are one nation under God, indivisible, with liberty and justice for all.*

many of us no longer study our history, which begs the question: Are we doomed to repeat it? Here are several pertinent quotations from leaders of the past who helped America become the greatest nation on earth:

Fear is the foundation of most governments; but it is so sordid and brutal a passion, and renders men in whose breasts it predominates so stupid and miserable, that Americans will not be likely to approve of any political institution which is founded on it.

— John Adams, *Thoughts on Government*, 1776

Government is instituted for the common good; for the protection, safety, prosperity, and happiness of the people; and not for profit, honor, or private interest of any one man, family, or class of men; therefore, the people alone have an incontestable, unalienable, and indefeasible right to institute government; and to reform, alter, or totally change the same, when their protection, safety, prosperity, and happiness require it.

— John Adams, *Thoughts on Government*, 1776

It is the duty of all men in society, publicly, and at stated seasons, to worship the Supreme Being, the great Creator and Preserver of the universe. And no subject shall be hurt, molested, or restrained, in his person, liberty, or estate, for worshipping God in the manner most agreeable to the dictates of his own conscience; or for his religious profession or sentiments; provided he doth not disturb the public peace, or obstruct others in their religious worship.

— John Adams, *Thoughts on Government*, 1776

I now make it my earnest prayer, that God would have you, and the State over which you preside, in his holy protection, that he would incline the hearts of the Citizens to cultivate a spirit of subordination and obedience to Government, to entertain a brotherly affection and love for one another, for their fellow Citizens of the United States at large, and particularly for their brethren who have served in the Field, and finally, that he would most graciously be pleased to dispose us all, to do Justice, to love mercy, and to demean ourselves with that Charity, humility, and pacific temper of mind, which were the Characteristics of the Divine Author of our blessed Religion, and without an humble imitation of whose example in these things, we can never hope to be a happy Nation.

— George Washington, *Circular Letter of Farewell to the Army*, June 8, 1783

Faith Triumphs in Trouble

Every difference of opinion is not a difference of principle. We have called by different names brethren of the same principle.

— Thomas Jefferson, *First Inaugural Address,*
March 4, 1801

Darkness cannot drive out darkness; only light can do that. Hate cannot drive out hate; only love can do that. Hate multiplies hate, violence multiplies violence, and toughness multiplies toughness in a descending spiral of destruction. ... The chain reaction of evil—hate begetting hate, wars producing more wars—must be broken, or we shall be plunged into the dark abyss of annihilation.

— Martin Luther King, Jr., *Strength To Love,*
1963

The Church must be reminded that it is not the master or the servant of the State, but rather the conscience of the State. It must be the guide and the critic of the State, and never its tool. If the Church does not recapture its prophetic zeal, it will become an irrelevant social club without moral or spiritual authority.

— Martin Luther King, Jr., *Strength to Love,*
1963

Power at its best is love implementing the demands of justice. Justice at its best is love correcting everything that stands against love.

— Martin Luther King, Jr., *Where Do We Go from Here: Chaos or Community?* 1967

The church was not merely a thermometer that recorded the ideas and principles of popular opinion; it was a thermostat that transformed the mores of society.

— Martin Luther King, Jr., *Speech at Civil Rights March on Washington,* August 28, 1963

Bishop Eddie Long is the pastor of New Birth Baptist Church, with more than twenty thousand members, in Lithonia, Georgia, a suburb of Atlanta. Long had the privilege of working with Coretta Scott King, the widow of Dr. Martin Luther King, Jr., and matriarch of the surviving King family. In fact, the moving funeral service for Mrs. King was held at New Birth. The event drew a sitting president, former presidents, and dignitaries from around the world. On that day, they looked beyond politics and race and urged the world to consider the example of Coretta Scott King and her late husband Martin. They also called on the world to establish a legacy of faith, hope, and love.

Continuing on that legacy of fostering hope, one of the messages that Bishop Long often shares is on the topic of generational transfer. The news media and members of

Congress have discussed in great detail the transfer of debt to future generations. In other words, the budgets that are made today will have to be paid by the generations of tomorrow. The same principle applies to our spiritual development. What we teach our children about loving God today will be passed on to our children's children. For that reason, Bishop Long urges people to grasp the truth written in God's Word. He discusses how there is a difference between those who trust in their heart and those who trust in God. He explains that those who trust in God are not moved by the trends and shifts of circumstances in the world.

"The economy does not shake them. They are not anxious, worried, or afraid," says Long. In pointing out the difference between the two opposing thoughts, he adds, "Everyone who trusts in their heart is caught up in things that cause despair."

The news media and members of Congress have discussed in great detail the transfer of debt to future generations. In other words, the budgets that are made today will have to be paid by the generations of tomorrow. The same principle applies to our spiritual development.

A good man ... will never be shaken ... .
His heart is steadfast, trusting in the LORD.
His heart is established; he will not be afraid.

Psalm 112:5-8

Long adds,

When your heart is filled with doubt, you cannot obey God and walk in obedience in order for God to bless you. In Matthew 17:20, Jesus says, *"If you have faith ... , you will say to this mountain, 'Move from here to there,' and it will move."* All things that you speak and ask in faith, and believe shall come to pass. The time to really believe God is when you're under pressure, when troubles are hitting you from the left and the right. That's when you've got to believe and not doubt. Don't ever doubt. Faith is boundless and timeless. There are no boundaries; faith transcends time.

By adopting true faith in God, we are able to transfer from generation to generation the kind of faith that will impact the world. Jesus provided an example of this when He gave His final instructions to His disciples before ascending into heaven. In Mark 16:15, He told the eleven disciples, *"Go into all the world and preach the gospel to every creature."*

Faith Triumphs in Trouble

Jesus sent His disciples on a mission to have a global impact. However, He first trained them to do more than just going around broadcasting the good news about the kingdom. He instructed them on the strategies to make a lasting impact on the world. *The National Catholic Reporter* published a commentary on this chapter and verse, highlighting ways the disciples exercised their faith with impact. It cited the following:

> One way is through followers of Christ who live out the gospel and proclaim it to the world. That's why the lifestyles and relationships of believers are so important. People are watching to see how we, as Christians, handle our responsibilities and resources. Is there any evidence that Christ really makes a difference in our lives?
> Another way is through Christian institutions, such as local churches, parachurch organizations, and the Christian media ... . You have an important opportunity to touch the needs of the world with Christ's love and power.
> A third sphere of influence is through lobbying and advocacy ... . Attempt to influence the institutions and people that control society.
> — *National Catholic Reporter,* October 27, 1989

Of course, this means that every follower of Jesus Christ should understand that we do not receive a free pass from participating in this experience called life. We can activate our faith and introduce it to the world by the way we speak, act, and show our love for our fellowman. We can do something as simple as voting for the candidate of our choice based on our belief. We can even run for office or become a grassroots community leader who works to help people improve their lives. In essence, it's important for followers of Jesus Christ to understand that they can touch the world by meeting people at their point of need.

This, my friends, is *America's Hope*.

Chapter Twelve

Together We Can Change the World

The LORD will mediate between nations
and will settle international disputes.
They will hammer their swords into plowshares
and their spears into pruning hooks.
Nation will no longer fight against nation,
nor train for war anymore.   Isaiah 2:4, NLT

In this book, I have shared some of my insights with you. No doubt, some things you understand and possibly agree with, but there are other subjects you do not agree with or comprehend. That's fine. It will provide room for discussion on various issues such as faith, hope, and love. What is clear is this: We have to rise up and overcome the problems within the economy, politics, culture, and race. All of these topics require further dialogue, which, I hope, will prove to be fruitful.

Here's one thing I hope we all can agree on: Without

> *I believe it is imperative that we learn to govern from a love for God, our neighbors and our world. After all, what have we got to lose? We have tried everything else, and we still have the same problems confronting us.*

faith in God, it will be impossible to find healing. Without faith, it will be difficult to find solutions to our global problems. I hope we all can agree that without faith in God there can be no real sustainable hope, which we need so desperately. Furthermore, I hope we all can agree that without faith, without hope, there can be no love. That, my friends, would be disastrous. Love enables us to endure all things, bear all things, and overcome all things.

I understand that love is a four-letter word that is seldom used in government and politics these days. Yet I believe it is imperative that we learn to govern from a love for God, our neighbors, and our world. After all, what have we got to lose? We have tried everything else, and we still have the same problems confronting us. World leaders, renowned world economists, and members of the major think tanks have all failed to develop a strategy that everyone can agree on. The global debate about how to end the economic crisis, stop the wars, and end hunger and poverty still rages on.

Perhaps the little church in Greencastle, the volunteers serving at the Boys & Girls Club of Statesboro, the volunteer soldiers providing food and clothing for the poor in Iraq, the men and women working toward racial reconciliation through the power of forgiveness, and so many other people not mentioned in this book have the right idea.

Can you imagine all politicians checking their egos and partisanship at the door because they love each other enough to govern, not from the Left, not from the Right, but from a moral center? Yes, I know there would still be disagreements on a multitude of issues, but there would be a more harmonious approach to finding common ground on every one of them.

The fruit of that kind of legislating might not make headlines or the lead story on network or local news. What? No conflict? No dirty laundry? No verbal fireworks to report? Who would watch our news shows, read our headlines, or listen to our radio talk-show hosts frothing at the mouth? How will we achieve great ratings or increase our viewers, listeners, and readers without controversy? Trust me! There will always be enough news out there to capture the people's attention. The difference might be an opportunity for reporting on stories that would be more focused on programs, ideas, and people who are involved in finding solutions, stories that inspire and motivate more of us to volunteer, to offer our services wherever or whenever we're needed.

I can only imagine that many people would find such reporting very uplifting and encouraging. To all my news colleagues, forgive me for my frankness on this issue, but suppose there's a chance that news organizations could adopt this positive approach to looking at an issues and then addressing it with a tone of "we're all in this mess together, so here are some positive suggestions on how we can address it and clean it up together." Imagine politicians, business leaders, news media, clergy, and we the people, all of us working together to tackle each challenge that comes our way, without the doom and gloom and constant chatter of how bad things are. Let's be honest and acknowledge the bad, but let's not be afraid to place more emphasis on what's good and what's right in our world and with our fellowman.

There is power in accentuating the positive. It is liberating and exhilarating to feel the rush of faith, hope, and love coursing through your thoughts. It makes you feel powerful enough to believe that you can say to any mountain of problems, "Be removed," and before your very eyes, it will literally become a molehill and dissolve into nothingness.

Faith in God provides us with the incredible ability to love without fear, to never be subjected to that kind of bondage. It enables us to live our lives free of worry, and to be full of trust and confidence.

After spending all of this time with me, reading the pages

of this tome, I hope you feel as if you can dare to dream, dare to believe, and dare to love. I trust that you have hope in your hope, faith in your faith, and love in your love.

The power of love is an awesome miracle that God blesses us with each day that we live. It compels us to look beyond our circumstances and see heaven, beyond the trials and travails we experience here on earth. I'm so glad trouble doesn't last forever, and I'm so glad that God promises He will never leave us or forsake us.

Please understand and know that I am always praying for you, whether you are the President of the United States, a member of Congress, a man or woman serving a life sentence in prison, a person who is homeless, or whatever other position you may currently have in life. Please know that while I love you with all of my human frailty, God loves you even more in the fullness of His glory. He shows His love to us through the cross of Calvary, where Jesus willingly allowed Himself to be crucified in exchange for our sins. He did this through His infinite love for us, knowing that by His death and resurrection we could have the forgiveness of our sins and the blessed assurance of having a joyful eternity with Him.

Let God's love cover the multitude of grievances and offenses we may have committed against each other. I pray that we decide to live the love life, loving God with all of our heart and soul, and loving our neighbor as much as we love ourselves.

Please understand that no matter where you've been or

what you've done, God is always near, and He hears every prayer. He will always answer you. He promises that He will never leave you or forsake you. I'm convinced that no matter what trials we face (even when the storms of life come upon us suddenly and without warning), God will be there for us. Through the tears you cry, through your pain, your sorrow, and even your fear, He will be there. I know that God will carry you out of your "mess," turn your "mess" into a message, and enable you to deliver that message as a messenger of God's love.

I understand that some of you may have read these pages more out of curiosity than anything else. "How far will he go in proclaiming that Jesus is the answer for the world today?" you might be thinking to yourself, and you may come to the conclusion that I'm too deeply involved in "this Jesus thing." Well, I thank you for reading the book thus far, but I also know that some of you are wondering how you can possess more faith in Jesus Christ. Can you trust Him with all of your heart? Looking at the world and its troubles, it would be easy for me to complain, but that wouldn't change a thing. I have found that trusting God, exercising my faith in Jesus, and acting on the power of the gospel through the Holy Spirit makes me strong enough to endure the complexities of life. God's ways are not my ways, so I have learned to cling to every principle and strategy of His Word.

Now, that doesn't make me a man bordering on religious fanaticism. Quite the contrary! I assure you that I am quite sane and rational. But I have found the true secret of living a successful life. For those of you who are tired of trying to go through life on your own, please allow me the honor of introducing you to the greatest Person you could ever meet, our Lord and Savior Jesus Christ.

First, please understand that the gospel of Jesus Christ is more than just personal; it is also public. It can help you in every area of your life, good and evil, success or failure, science and technology, public policy, racial reconciliation, international relations, economics, parenthood, sadness and joy ... everything under the sun. The beauty of God's holiness and righteousness is that He cares about you. He knows your name. He knew you before you were even conceived and placed in your mother's womb. He knows your every thought, your hurt, your fears, and your hopes and dreams. He loves you so much that He hears you when you call on

The gospel of Jesus Christ is more than just personal; it is also public. It can help you in every area of your life, good and evil, success or failure, science and technology, public policy, racial reconciliation, international relations, economics, parenthood, sadness and joy ... everything under the sun.

Him for any reason. So join me now in calling on Him to hear this sincere prayer for salvation:

Lord, I acknowledge that in this world, there is none righteous, no, not one, for all have sinned and fall short of the glory of God. But, Lord, the Bible tells me, in Romans 10:8-10:

"The word is near you, in your mouth and in your heart' ... : that if you confess with your mouth the Lord Jesus and believe in your heart that God has raised Him from the dead, you will be saved. For with the heart one believes unto righteousness, and with the mouth confession is made unto salvation."

The Scriptures say that whoever believes on Him will *"not be put to shame"* (Psalm 25:20, NIV), and *"Whoever calls on the name of the LORD shall be saved"* (Joel 2:32). So, Lord, I humbly ask You to forgive me of my sins. Forgive my unbelief. I welcome You into my heart as my Lord, Savior, and Friend.

If you said this prayer with me, you are now born again. From this day forward, develop your faith by studying the Bible. Find a good Bible-teaching church where you can worship with fellow believers in Jesus Christ and study to grow in your faith. Welcome to salvation, to a life of fullness of joy, even in the midst of a troubled world. So, dear friend, come enjoy the incredible privilege of knowing that you are a friend of God.

> *Come, Holy Spirit, shine your holy light; lead me*
> *out of darkness.*
> *Shine your holy light; lift me out of bondage.*
> *Shine your holy light; let me see salvation.*
> *Shine your holy light; deliver your creation.*
>
> Kelly Wright

Now be joyful and know that whom the Son sets free is free indeed!

So this is our purpose: We must walk in love. We must be careful how we treat each other. Every day of our lives, we should seek to be a people of grace and truth, not as rude and obnoxious as possible. We should share our joy with a world that is filled with sorrow. Let us aspire to take time to share the love that Christ placed inside of us with a world that is consumed by hate. Let them see the real Jesus in us.

Beyond politics, beyond race, beyond war, and beyond all troubles, there is a greater destination for all of us who trust in God. Therefore, let us lovingly spread His message of hope in these times of despair.

This, my friends, is *America's Hope in Troubled Times*.

The Believer's Manifesto

While Americans can boast of having created the U.S. Constitution (which I believe is the greatest document forged by any government ever), let us not forget that God has forged a document that helps all of us to govern our hearts, minds, and souls. This document, known as The Beatitudes, was authored by Jesus Christ Himself, while delivering His famous Sermon on the Mount.

Matthew 5:

You're Blessed

[1-2] *When Jesus saw his ministry drawing huge crowds, he climbed a hillside. Those who were apprenticed to him, the committed, climbed with him. Arriving at a quiet place, he sat down and taught his climbing companions. This is what he said:*

[3] *"You're blessed when you're at the end of your rope. With less of you there is more of God and his rule.*

[4] *"You're blessed when you feel you've lost what is most dear to you. Only then can you be embraced by the One most dear to you.*

[5] *"You're blessed when you're content with just who you are—no more, no less. That's the moment you find yourselves proud owners of everything that can't be bought.*

[6] *"You're blessed when you've worked up a good appetite*

222

for God. He's food and drink in the best meal you'll ever eat.

⁷ *"You're blessed when you care. At the moment of being 'care-full,' you find yourselves cared for.*

⁸ *"You're blessed when you get your inside world—your mind and heart—put right. Then you can see God in the outside world.*

⁹ *"You're blessed when you can show people how to cooperate instead of compete or fight. That's when you discover who you really are, and your place in God's family.*

¹⁰ *"You're blessed when your commitment to God provokes persecution. The persecution drives you even deeper into God's kingdom.*

¹¹⁻¹² *"Not only that—count yourselves blessed every time people put you down or throw you out or speak lies about you to discredit me. What it means is that the truth is too close for comfort and they are uncomfortable. You can be glad when that happens—give a cheer, even!— for though they don't like it, I do! And all heaven applauds. And know that you are in good company. My prophets and witnesses have always gotten into this kind of trouble."*

Salt and Light

¹³ *"Let me tell you why you are here. You're here to be salt-seasoning that brings out the God-flavors of this earth. If you lose your saltiness, how will people taste*

godliness? You've lost your usefulness and will end up in the garbage.

14-16 *"Here's another way to put it: You're here to be light, bringing out the God-colors in the world. God is not a secret to be kept. We're going public with this, as public as a city on a hill. If I make you light-bearers, you don't think I'm going to hide you under a bucket, do you? I'm putting you on a light stand. Now that I've put you there on a hilltop, on a light stand—shine! Keep open house; be generous with your lives. By opening up to others, you'll prompt people to open up with God, this generous Father in heaven."*

Completing God's Law

17-18 *"Don't suppose for a minute that I have come to demolish the Scriptures—either God's Law or the Prophets. I'm not here to demolish but to complete. I am going to put it all together, pull it all together in a vast panorama. God's Law is more real and lasting than the stars in the sky and the ground at your feet. Long after stars burn out and earth wears out, God's Law will be alive and working.*

19-20 *"Trivialize even the smallest item in God's Law and you will only have trivialized yourself. But take it seriously, show the way for others, and you will find honor in the kingdom. Unless you do far better than the Pharisees in the matters of right living, you won't know the first thing about entering the kingdom."*

The Message